Cut The Strings

Cut The Strings

The True Story of a Soul Reclaimed

Lynn Grocott

First Published In Great Britain 2005
by www.BookShaker.com

Typeset in Georgia

For my husband Glen, and my three beautiful daughters Kristy, Emma and Alison. It is with their constant love and support this book has been written

CONTENTS

FOREWORD

As a mountaineer I'm often faced with a series of challenges I have to overcome in order to reach the summit – my eventual goal. By taking on such an adventure you simply accept that there will be mishaps, problems, fears and obstacles to overcome on your journey. And, you do your very best, through planning and preparation, to ensure none of them are critical always aware that some things, like the weather and nature, are simply beyond control.

Well life – possibly the greatest adventure of all – is like that too. We all have goals, ambitions and dreams. We all have our own personal summits – sometimes vivid – sometimes vague. And, inevitably there will be obstacles to face and overcome. Some of these obstacles will be personal challenges, inner demons, that we need to conquer. Other obstacles, we simply have no choice about and it's how we then respond to them that can mean the difference between eventual success or early defeat.

How do you face and overcome your personal fears? What do you do when fate deals you a bad hand? How can you respond to your own "bad luck" and "misfortune" to turn it around?

In this very personal story and guidebook, Lynn Grocott shares what she's learned as one of life's less–than–lucky adventurers to make the path a little more passable for those who follow.

Sir Chris Bonington
www.bonington.com

PREFACE

Personal Growth is a term that is pushed around with the greatest of ease these days and as such can become diluted. I am therefore reluctant to use the term in connection with Lynn Grocott. Let me explain.

The first time that I was aware of Lynn's existence was in September 2004. She was a delegate at the same conference as me. I had seen her during some of the conference sessions and noticed her determination to get involved despite having to rely on arm crutches to move round the conference facilities.

On the third morning of the conference, Lynn took over the proceedings as she walked unaided to the stage, demanding to make a short speech. I will not go into the details of the speech here except to say that it was delivered with such emotion that, although the day's proceedings were only a few minutes old, the organiser called a time out.

Through my own tear blotched eyes, I saw delegates having their own, individual emotional clearing either staring out of the windows or just hugging each other.

That morning was, in my opinion, the beginning of Lynn's spiralling growth. Within a few days, she completed a two mile, non stop swim.

Since returning from that conference, I have seen Lynn swim three miles and her aim is to swim the equivalent of the English channel.

Since January 2005, Lynn has been in and out of hospital for tests on a mystery illness that has confounded doctors. This illness has put a temporary stop to her swimming. On the positive side, it has given

Lynn time to find even more inner strength to complete her first book, become a broadcaster and help others where she can.

On average, I visit Lynn once per week at her home near Uttoxeter and am always greeted by a warm smile and a woman that bounces across the room, often to the detriment of the cup of tea that is always on offer. On these occasions, I try to visualise, how much energy she would have if the medical profession could treat her mystery illness.

Throughout this period of character intensification, Lynn has been supported by her family. In particular, her husband Glen without whom, Lynn would not have grown so rapidly, if at all.

So this is why I am reluctant to call it personal growth in the traditional, watered down sense. I would rather describe it as Character Intensification brought about by using her inner resources and fully supported by Glen.

Bryn Jones

Motivator, Mentor, Professional Speaker
and proud friend to Lynn and Glen Grocott.

Introduction

Many times before we read a book we need to ask ourselves is this book for me? Will I enjoy it? Will it strike a chord? Well let me ask you... Are you travelling in a direction at the moment and wondering where you're going? Or why you are travelling in that direction at all? Are you searching for something but are unsure why you are longing for more? Are you suffering in a situation, perhaps feeling like a victim, without knowing where to turn or where to go for help? Well it could be this book is for you. It follows my journey to find self worth.

Whilst travelling its many pages you will be taken on a trip full of fear. You will meet with the darker side of life, from childhood abuse and suicide through to anorexia and mental instability. You will find out about life's challenges but most of all you will discover triumph and hope.

You may even discover an idea which may be thought–provoking enough to have an impact on your own life and change things for the better.

So, now you know what the book may offer, it's up to you. It is You Who Must Decide to read on.

This book does not ask for your sympathy, dear reader; its aim is to show you that you can overcome *anything* in life. Absolutely nothing need hold you back. Even if now you feel like a victim, you can be a winner, turning unspeakable sexual and physical abuse, violence, deprivation and heartbreak into positive thought and action. We can all become winners instead of victims. We can learn to empower ourselves. We can become aware that we are all unique individuals with something to offer to the world. What is more we owe it to ourselves to discover how magnificent we truly are.

I hope to illustrate to you that each human being has an incredible strength, and the vast resources to cope with anything that hinders happiness, peace and joy. I am not for one minute suggesting that by reading this book you will not face another challenge in your life, but hopefully you will be better equipped to deal with adversity when it rears its head.

This indeed is the story of cutting your strings. But I will keep you hanging in suspense for a moment until I reveal the reason for the title of this narrative.

ACKNOWLEDGEMENTS

The credit for the discovery of overcoming challenge and adversity in my life lies in the hands of many people but for me I would like to mention my beloved husband, Glen, my children and also a great and dear friend Tony Burgess.

My family surround me at all times with love and support. They have seen me through some harrowing things and had to live with me as I have learned to change. This has not been easy for them, and I know for certain that their own lives have been drastically affected because of the things which I am about to disclose to you.

I am still learning, and the journey is not over but their love remains strong and their loyalty amazing. There is no doubt that without their strength and encouragement my journey would have been so much harder, in fact truth be known I would not be where I am today. I love them dearly and cannot express to you how proud I am of each one of them.

1: STRINGS

To show you how a shift in outlook can change you, I feel it is vitally important to share with you some of the things which have haunted me and caused me to be stagnant in my life for so many years. They have caused intense emotional pain and have at times caused me to feel like a victim. I have decided it would be best if I shared with you my story which reveals the process by which I became the person I am today.

I have learned that the most important purpose in life is to be happy. Happiness is a state of mind; and despite what goes on around us we get to choose how we feel about it. There have been many times in my life where I have seen fit to blame circumstance or people for my happiness – or lack thereof. I now realise I have control over my feelings. I can chose to sit and allow challenge to beat me, squash my zest for life, drive me to despair. Or I can look upon challenge in a different light; as an opportunity to learn something and to discover resources, already within me, to help me cope.

In the past adversity has led to many unhappy moments. I am not for one minute saying I welcome adversity with open arms, but I now have the ability to reason with the problem which is staring me in the face.

I have also learned that no matter what a person is finding difficult, the emotions involved are very similar; there comes panic, anger, fear, distress and so on. I hope this book will reach out to you, and make you realise *you* are more resourceful than you could ever imagine and that you can cope with all life throws at you. But more than that, you can, learn from it and put it to positive use. You don't have to be a victim.

I have learned the true value of happiness, it cannot be bought and it cannot come from other people. Happiness comes from accepting yourself, liking yourself and believing in yourself.

I also want you to see your own true worth; you have a part to play in this world. Whoever you are, you are an amazing individual. You have things to offer and you can always do and be more than you think you can. Dreams can become reality, it is just a question of whether you believe enough in yourself to be able to take the step of attaining your goals.

This is my story of breaking free from life as a victim and becoming an individual in my own right. It is my story of gaining happiness. It is a story that I hope will speak to your heart and help you to achieve your goals too. If it helps you get more from your own life then it has served its purpose. You are an amazing individual and you deserve happiness.

My husband thought of a title for this story and it is something I want to share with you, "The Pinocchio Syndrome". As time goes on I hope you will realise the relevance of such a title. Let us think for a moment of the puppet Pinocchio. He was carved out of wood and longed to be free. He felt tied by his strings to his master and knew he had an individual within him bursting to be master of his own destiny. He did not want to be forever controlled by the strings, the pulling of the master's hand, the control over his every action. This analogy is so apt to the story of abuse because the abuser becomes like a puppeteer whilst the child becomes the equivalent of the puppet.

The master pulls the strings, operating the puppet with such a sense of power and complete control. He becomes a ventriloquist at times speaking through the mouth of the child he is tormenting. How many cases can you recall where the child has been forced to say "everything is alright?" The events I am going to recount to you, are typical examples of this inhibiting control.

2: House of Horrors

I begin with my earliest memories. They are not pleasant to recall.

I remember the street in which I grew up, it was a terraced row of houses, I think now of the front door in Stoke on Trent and how it shone. Mum wiped the dust from the traffic away each day, demonstrating to the world what a house–proud woman she was. The windows gleamed as she cleaned them each morning always at the same time of day, sometimes, in the cold and dark as winter mornings turned from black to grey.

However, this was done to create an illusion; as the entrance opened its mouth to the house of horrors. A house filled with deep dark secrets that belong in a horror movie.

Inside, to the naked eye, was the usual layout of front room, living room, kitchen and then two bedrooms sat upstairs. The walls to this day hold so many stories. The ceiling groans with distaste and the extra small room, which is just big enough for one to stand up and shake in, must now feel so relieved to be free of the sounds which would penetrate its inner walls. No bathroom or shower could be found within the house, bathing would take place at the kitchen sink and once each week I would go to my Gran's house for a hot bath. The toilet was a separate concrete building outside in the yard – freezing cold on winter days and dark during the night–time.

No one could ever criticise dad for not working hard. He was an upholsterer by trade and how pride oozed from his very soul over his work. People would call upon him to repair, recover and even make their three piece suites, chairs and sofas. He would lovingly work on the chosen piece making sure each item was finished to the highest standard.

So here was a man with such pride, a man in his late twenties who could create a beautiful item from nothing. However, the truth of the matter was...

My dad was a monster in the true sense of the word! Perhaps you are thinking, "So what, we have all experienced times when our parents did not live up to our expectations." But let me explain further and you will see what I mean.

The first vivid memory I have is of being in my cot. I am standing and crying. I feel thirsty and I want a drink of water. It is so dark in this room. Dad comes in. He throws me down and tells me to wait till morning. That I am just being greedy. I wait and wait and wait hoping for water. None comes. I go to sleep thirsty – GREEDY – a word which has resounded in my ears for years to come.

Mum worked at a bakery and I was looked after during the week by my wonderful grandmother. When I was old enough to go to school my grandmother used to collect me from the bottom of the street where she lived. She always had a smile on her face. She was an inspiration in the true sense of the word and I have seen times when she would have ten of my friends around the house to play and to stay to tea. She had very little in the way of material things but she made people smile so much. She would invent games and make dens with me.

My grandmother was my dad's mum, she had no other children, and I was the only grandchild. She had the most lovely silvery, white hair, which was so tightly packed with curls. Her hands were rough showing the signs of someone who had worked hard all her life.

Gran's dressing up box was wonderful; it was so good to put the masks and disguises on. When I dressed up I was transported in my mind to many far off places. I imagined I was free, I always had a happy place to go.

Sometimes I was a bride, pulling out the dress, trying it on and slipping into another world was so easy. My favourite outfit to wear though was my football strip. I can feel the excitement now as I pulled on the shirt, I imagined I was Gordon Banks, a once famous goal keeper who played for Stoke City and for England. I could feel my pride growing as I picked up my football and carried it onto the lawn. The grass soon became the turf in a football stadium; it felt wonderful under my feet, the smell was amazing, rich, clean, and how it glistened in the sun. The borders became the stands of the stadium, the plants and flowers became my cheering army of fans.

I was warming up, waiting for our captain to take the ball to the centre line, then the whistle would blow and the crowds would cheer. In my day–dream I was the most important person in the whole world. I would save the game. I would kick the ball up into the air and catch it. "SAVE!" I would shout. Then suddenly Gran's voice would bring me out of my dreams – my secret sanctuary. She would be calling me to say it was time to go and meet the real devil in my life. It was time to go and meet dad as he had finished work.

Time to come back to the real harsh world. In reality I was no Gordon Banks on my way to my next match, rather I was a terrified tormented child who was on her way home to face a beating in the wrestling ring. Yes, I was off to wrestling. Another mask was to be put on. Hoping it would not be long before the bell would ring so I could be saved from my opponent and off to bed.

Bed, how that one word can bring back some feelings, such as warmth, comfort, the enveloping of the sheets... so soft. But even those warm feelings were marred, as the bed could bring back other memories that were not so pleasant.

Dad used to drop me off on his way to work and collect me from my Gran as he finished his shift. We always got home before my mum. I used to wear a white vest under my top layer of clothing and white pants. Every day when we got home dad insisted on a game of wrestling. He called my vest my "shimmy", I don't know why, but that word has stuck with me for all these years. We would start to wrestle, such fun at first, but then he would say, "Take your shimmy off and you will look like a proper wrestler". Can you imagine being told as a child you would look like a wrestler, how thrilling, how exciting, how proud... but no. All my tiny scarred mind felt was fear and panic. Each day I wondered if I was stronger than the day before. Would he catch the bit which was still painful from my last round with him?

I did as he told me. I could feel my knees shaking, my arms felt weak, maybe today would be different, maybe he was right, he was doing this for my own good. I looked down at my legs and tensed the non–existent muscles on my arms. Yes, that was it, I needed muscle, he was right, this was a way to get muscle.

Maybe I was weak and I needed to toughen up so that I wouldn't be picked on when I was at school. Maybe if I did as I was told I would become a proper wrestler and be on the television when I grew up.

You have to earn whatever you get, I used to hear dad say. So I assumed that I'd earned the beatings too. Maybe, just maybe, I could become a wrestler and earn that too. I did need to be stronger and maybe that was the reason. Perhaps one day I would be glad he had done what he'd done.

Yes this was the way. If I reached a point where I no longer felt his punches and his blows, I would be a proper wrestler... See how he was manipulating my mind and twisting my thoughts?

Either I didn't get any stronger or he became more violent because the results remained the same during every session. He used to get so aggressive, I can still hear the pounding in my head as his fists hit and hit but I could not feel anything. I think I must have gone numb with fear and shock.

Before mum came home he would make me get dressed and he would treat me to sweets or maybe an ice cream. He was in total control – the puppet master. Mum couldn't understand why I wasn't hungry when she cooked tea. But it became easier to eat it than to attempt to refuse; anything for peace and quiet.

Better to just eat than face the barrage of criticisms from mom, "I spend all this time cooking and you, you, you ungrateful little... just eat it!"

I would force the food down, sometimes to the point of feeling sick. The puppet master was again in complete control. Me, I was the puppet, too afraid of the consequences of speaking out. My puppet master felt powerful and safe because he knew that if I said anything to anyone they wouldn't believe it. The consequences of speaking out, the rejection and the anger, were too scary – so I kept quiet.

Then the day came when he broke my wrist. We had started "toy fighting" when he slammed it against the fireplace. I cried out in such pain. I heard the crack of the bone. I tried to stop the tears, "don't cry, don't cry", I kept saying to myself. I bit into my lip and it bled as I clamped down hard with my teeth. At least it distracted me from the pain in my wrist.

The look on his face was terrible. He was grinning – he looked evil. No remorse, no sorrow – just glee. Then he shook me, and for the briefest moment there was a sense of panic in his eyes. He looked afraid. But I knew from past events that he was going to find his own dirty way out of this. What was he going to make me do now? Was he going to hit me for getting hurt, was he going to scream at me, or was I going to get a "cuddle" in the full meaning of what that word meant to him. Not too bad this time, I got away lightly really. All that happened was that I was forced to say that I had been sliding up the garden in the snow, and had fallen over hitting it on a curbstone.

He made me wait from Saturday until Monday before going to the hospital because he told me there was nothing wrong with it. You see, he was so wrapped up in his Horse Racing on the television on a Saturday afternoon that no one dared speak. Nothing could take priority over his race. He used to sit on his chair staring at the television, glass of whiskey in hand. He would move to the edge of his seat as the horse he had gambled on ran its race. I can see him now, "Go on boy ... go on!" he would shout. And when he lost, the atmosphere would be like ice. I could even see the worry in my mum's eyes but I cannot make any assumption as to what occurred between the two of them.

During those two days, I lay awake at night time. My wrist and hand swelled up so much that even my knuckles were changing colour. He came into my bedroom on the Saturday evening, "Let's have a look then, you seem to be making a lot of fuss over nothing! He looked at it, then reached out his hand to touch it. I knew even before he did it that he would bring more pain. He lifted it turned it over and over, squeezing it in all the different places he could find.

Then he let it drop from his hand onto my knee. I tried so hard not to cry, the tears were welling up. "Please stop, please stop," I thought but the tears spilled out and then SLAP! His hand on the side of my cheek as he snarled, "You cry baby... you big cry baby!" Then he looked sorry, for a split second I saw a quiver of guilt, he sat on the bed and whispered in my ear, "Would you like a cuddle? I thought I had got away without the cuddle, but no it was still to come. "Don't forget it is two headed llama night tonight." Now you just be good, or the llama won't bring your favourite sweets and that wouldn't be nice at all, would it?"

I felt physically sick from the pain. My head span round and round. I tried so hard not to think of what was in store. Not only pain from the arm but now the mental torture of what was in store for me. I was aching inside, thinking I must have been very bad to deserve this. What had I done that so wrong? I looked at myself in the mirror and, I really wondered if I was an awful child. Maybe this was all happening to me because I needed to learn to be good.

Monday came and mum was shouting at me because she had to miss a whole day off work to take me to the hospital with my wrist. She shouted at me for sliding up the garden. She raged about the cost of the taxi needed to take us to the hospital and back. At the hospital they gave me another appointment to have the plaster checked and I was subjected to even more recriminations for my clumsiness. How I longed to be able to tell the truth, but again my truth was stifled by the monster in my life. At the hospital they plastered it and it remained in plaster for weeks. So strange how much concern mum showed in front of the nurse!

The anger my dad expressed haunted me. It left me so afraid of such an emotion. The fear became distorted causing me to interpret even the smallest criticism as anger, or worse – rejection.

Once I was playing with my dolls which were all dressed in national costume. I was trying to make them sit on their knees. He told me to stop it as I would break the dolls. Before I had a chance to stop what I was doing he snatched the doll from my hand and then he chased me upstairs hitting me as we went up. I remember shouting "Daddy, please stop, please stop." But he just carried on until he had spent the anger that filled him. I felt so humiliated, and afraid, I could feel panic inside, I tried so hard not to sob because crying only led to him calling me a cry baby and saying, "If you don't shut up, I'll give you something to cry for!" His face used to turn white when he was angry and his eyes were full of venom, he almost resembled a cobra waiting for its prey.

I still wonder to this day, what it was that made dad so angry. I think something must have caused him great pain in his life to have such bitterness within him. Or was it that he had never experienced love in the true sense of the word? Surely, no one could possibly be like this without having *something* to explain such a controlling, aggressive streak in his personality.

You might recall the story of Dr Doolittle. There was an odd animal in it, a two headed Llama, otherwise known as the "Push–Me–Pull–You" Well, on Saturday nights, Dad would go to the local shop and buy some chocolate lime sweets. Even to this day I recall the taste, smell and appearance of these sweets. The image of them can still catch me unaware and leads to a feeling of panic. However, if it creeps in now, I am better equipped to deal with it; I can turn panic into a different emotion, one which is constructive instead of destructive, using the tools I have acquired during my healing process. You will read more about these tools as you read on but back to the Push–Me–Pull–You.

Dad's game would begin, he would bring a blanket down from upstairs and I would have to lie at one end of the settee with him at the other. In that respect he said that we were a, "two headed llama." He would pass sweets under the blanket but whilst doing that his hands would be all over my small body. I did not realise how wrong this was, all that I knew was that it felt uncomfortable in my mind and body.

Once again rewarded with sweets, I began to see this game as a means of comfort, of acceptance. My weight slowly crept up and up until at the age of nine I weighed ten stone. As an adult I'm only four feet ten and a half inches tall, so I was never designed to carry a vast amount of weight.

So, as a child I looked like a little barrel which led to more problems. I got bullied at school because of how heavy I was. And I was always the last one picked for school teams. The other children teased me and my nickname came to be Yeti (the abominable snowman).

What is so strange is that on Two Headed Llama nights mum would be in the same room watching the television. It was as though she knew what was happening but was too afraid to do anything about it. Or perhaps she just saw this as something which was quite natural. Other people have suggested that mum used me as a shield to avoid having to face my dad using and abusing her. But who knows what went on between them? I will never know and I for one cannot even begin to understand the reasoning behind her lack of action.

Then one Sunday morning mum *did* do something!! Dad always shouted me into his and mum's bed, a normal Sunday for me.

I walked slowly hands shaking, heart skipping beat after beat. I entered the room, so difficult to take in the surrounding furniture and the décor. The bed looked huge, but certainly not inviting! After all it was supporting the figure of the puppet master, as he beckoned me with that lustful look which told the story of what was to happen. The smell enveloped me as it always did, sweat, so strong it seemed to force its way onto my lips as I tried so hard to keep my mouth tightly shut. It forced its way into my nostrils, even though I held my breath. Feelings of nausea swept over me, my legs buckled as I made the short distance to the side of the bed. He drew his hand from under the covers, where he had already started his game some minutes before. The furniture was like that in a doll's house as it shrank into the distance, first the wardrobe then the chest of drawers, how I wished the wardrobe door would open up and allow me to escape into another world. His hand gripped my arm, as he drew me closer to the bed then I knew I was in his den, such confusion.

But on this occasion it was different, as I took my position the door opened and – mum came in and I was suddenly whisked away to stay at my grandparents for a while. I felt a combination of emotions. I was angry with my mum because I could not understand why she had stopped my dad from giving me a cuddle, some kind of physical affection, a love which I then thought was normal and natural.

I could not understand why it was so physically painful when he did what he did to me but I did not know any other type of love and I now felt rejected. I suddenly understood why he had told me to keep it a secret. This was exactly what he had warned me about. He said I would be punished. Why did she not want my dad to love me? Had I been too noisy when I went into their bedroom? Why had she come in? Why did she not want me in the house? No one spoke about what had happened.

My Gran acted as though nothing different had taken place, but then I don't really know what was talked about; I was on the side lines being moved around like a piece on a chess set. Dad would slip in for his tea at my Gran's after work on the odd evening for a week or so. I am not sure how long it was before I saw my mum again. The next time I saw my mum she had marks across her wrists. She said they were burns. When I look back, I realise now they were scars from deep, deep cuts.

Whenever I slept at my Gran's I would sleep in the spare room, I saw it as *my* room because I used it more than anyone. I can see it now. There was an old wooden bedroom suite in it. I have so many memories of the wardrobe. It had a secret compartment in the middle that moved around like a carrousel. I used to store so many secrets in here; it was my equivalent to the wardrobe in the classic book The Lion, The Witch and The Wardrobe.

I used to climb into the double bed which was my haven. No one could get to me in here. I would curl up under a heavy layer of blankets and a lovely soft flannelette sheet with a hot water bottle by my feet. What a fantastic feeling to know I could close my eyes and drift into a deep sleep without having to try and keep one ear listening for footsteps or the door handle moving.

But my happy thoughts about this bed were shattered in an instant...

Dad returned from the hospital, the night of July twenty first 1969. I remember the date because it was the day my brother was born.

I was ten years old. I once thought memories of that night would remain an unending nightmare, superimposed on any thought I would ever have again. I had played football with my granddad, had a bath, moved my secrets around in my drawer in the magical wardrobe, and crawled into bed tired but happy. I lay fast asleep in the warm double bed where I was safe. My hot water bottle giving off a gentle heat underneath my feet. How safe, how calm, how peaceful,

However, he had obviously worked his next move out, spied his chance and used the opportunity to fulfil his longings because Dad returned from the hospital, after mum had gone into labour.

"You have a baby brother but we don't know whether he will live or die. You see your mum and I have different blood groups and they have got to change his blood."

Then he climbed into bed. The physical pain, as he touched and penetrated me was awful. He was aggressive and so forceful, not gentle, no cuddle, instead he was like a dog foaming at the mouth wanting his prey. He showed no sense of remorse. It just came so easy to him.

As time went on mum used to say she'd had a miscarriage twelve months after I was born because she had carried buckets of water up and down the garden to try to get rid of the child. She also said she'd done the same when she was pregnant with me! She had not wanted a child. She hadn't wanted me.

As I got older I made every attempt to stay away from the house. Mum's story was repeated over and over again, she was not making it up, she really meant what she was saying. I felt uncomfortable at home. It's sad to say it but that home did not feel like home to me. I did not belong somehow. I can't remember ever playing with mum, not even a board game.

During the school holidays I would frequently sit in the local library, staring out of the reference room window. Anything was better than being where I wasn't wanted. I would spend endless nights with my grandparents or at my aunt's.

When I think about the fun I've had with my own children, the playing we have done together – I feel sorry for her. Poor old mum never had this experience and the truth was that she did not know how to be a child.

When I was about 16 my mum told me that I was not my dad's daughter but my grandfather's and that *he* had raped her. I did not know what to think or believe, was this true or was it her way of detaching herself from any guilt about all that had happened to me?

3: ESCAPE ATTEMPTS

School for me, I suppose was an average experience. On the whole I enjoyed it, apart from the times I was bullied for my weight. There were times when I tried too hard to be accepted and instead of attracting friends I caused them to pull away from me. I lacked encouragement from anyone to achieve anything. Truth be known I longed to be a teacher but my parents insisted I was not clever enough to do this. Staying on in the sixth form to do A levels was not talked about. It was assumed that I would leave school at the age of sixteen and go out to work.

However, I knew that I wanted to do a job that involved working with people in a caring capacity. So with lots of fuss it was agreed at the age of sixteen, I should attend a local sixth form college to undertake a course entitled Preliminary Residential Care. It entailed both a theoretical structure and placements in residential situations, involving work experience with the elderly, children and those suffering with mental illness and learning disabilities. I found my placements with the elderly helped me to build up confidence, with people.

During this time my passion for Sociology grew. I would feel my heart racing as I took in the theories. This was the first time my academic ability was recognised. I thrived and was so pleased when my report showed four A grades, one B grade and good grades for both Sociology and English O level.

But dad was not a happy man. He asked where the other A grade was. I felt demoralised, worthless, and as though nothing was ever going to be good enough to gain the love and affection I craved from my parents.

I began to fear them in so many ways. Every effort on my part was done to avoid them. I was searching for freedom, just like Pinocchio, what I didn't know at that time was that my insecurity and constant searching for acceptance would not lead me to where I wanted or needed to be. I was unable to find anyone who loved me properly. I met up with people whom I put my trust in but who would soon let me down.

They would promise the earth, I would believe them, and they would let me down. Hurt and suffering came hand in hand. I searched for love, for a sense of belonging but I was looking in all the wrong places. Once again I can see the similarities between myself and Pinocchio. I searched everywhere, allowing other people to pull my strings. I was dependent not in–dependent. My striving led to total unhappiness.

I just *had* to get away! The only way I could see to do this was to join the armed forces. I got accepted to join the air force to take up the trade of a nurse – my intake would start a few months later. In the interim period I worked on the geriatric unit at a local hospital, it was an amazing experience and I was to later regret not staying to undertake my general nurse training. But I had to escape the domestic situation at my parental home, so off I went to Hereford to begin my basic training.

I really enjoyed this part of my life. I was allowed to have a sense of belonging because the forces ensure that trainees develop as a team; it becomes necessary to remain strong emotionally as individuals and as a unit. We shared so many tears and so much laughter. I could not march to save my life and I was known for tripping myself up as I tried to co–ordinate my steps. It was fun, fun like I had not known before.

But discharge was to occur within three months due to asthma – the tears flowed. I was just beginning to feel as though I belonged somewhere and now it was a trip back to the so–called "family home". What was I going to do for a living? I had no idea where to start looking and no one was there to offer advice.

I couldn't see a way out. The walls felt as though they were closing in on me.

The only escape that I could see was to apply for civilian nurse training. I applied to anywhere with a school of nursing and the all important nurse's home. I was so disheartened after applying to several hospitals because the intakes were so far away. The only immediate offer was a hospital that catered for people with severe learning disabilities.

I was elated to have found somewhere, and therefore, quickly packed and moved into room eleven. I was soon out of my depth, and it became obvious that this field of care was not for me. I had done a placement working with disability but nothing could have prepared me for what I was to see.

My first ward was one which catered for severely mentally handicapped males. Thirty four of them in total. One of the men was capable of lifting himself, and the chair he was sitting in, off the floor for a seemingly endless number of repetitions without stopping. His physical strength was something to behold.

Physical strength never seemed to be inhibited. This was the same in a vast number of the patients; they simply didn't put restrictions upon themselves.

I found it difficult to accept the cards these people had been dealt; the elderly have had their lives. Residential care, as long as it is *good* care can allow the client a place to live in safety, with company and twenty four hour help available. The people at this hospital ranged from young children to adults – men and women. I can remember one young man who smiled when he was fed rice pudding but at any other time his expression remained blank. Some of the women were in this place due to having illegitimate children, they were scarred with the label of moral defect in years gone by. By the time I came to be doing my training they were so institutionalised there was little or no hope of ever integrating them into everyday society.

And so, images of the past caught up with me along with the pressure of being in an unsuitable demanding vocation, it was not long before I began to suffer all the signs of a complete nervous breakdown.

4: BREAKDOWN & MARRIAGE

I was now eighteen years old, feeling vulnerable and alone, afraid and insecure. I did not feel that I belonged anywhere and I certainly did not know who I was or even what I really wanted to do with my life.

It was at this point that Glen (now my wonderful husband) came into my life. He also lived in the nurses' home. He was amazing. Fortunately he was eleven years older than myself, had an enormous amount of experience of life, and slowly I began to trust him. In one way besides becoming a partner he became the father figure that I longed to have.

He was divorced and had three beautiful children from his first marriage, and I am now so proud to say that I am a grandmother. His compassion and understanding surpassed anything that I had ever experienced. His love demanded nor asked for anything in return, and we were soon to move into our first rented flat in 1979.

But the demons of my past had left me so insecure and so afraid of losing him. I constantly thought that he would find someone else and leave me alone to cope with the emptiness inside me. How could I expect this man to stand by me when I was so possessive, so demanding. I feared him being out of my sight to such an extent I would even hide in the boot of the car to prevent him going to work without me. I could not leave the house without him and catching any form of public transport was out of the question.

I felt a fear so intense that everything was irrational. I cannot begin to put into words what was going on inside. To anyone on the outside looking in I was totally disturbed.

I imagine you're thinking, "This woman must be mad, insane off her rocker." But this was the intensity of the scarring on my personality and my mind. I took overdoses and was admitted to a psychiatric ward.

It was so cold and so grey on the ward. A long dormitory to sleep in, people walking around not knowing how they were ever going to put their lives back together. Symptoms being masked by strong drugs. Some people had angry outbursts others simply walked around as if in a trance. The majority of the people were elderly – some were incontinent.

I looked into the eyes of some and you could see their anguish, feel their lack of hope, in some cases even the loss of dignity. I huddled in a chair in corner shaking, terrified, trying to avoid contact with anyone. I would keep my eyes lowered in case they made contact with the eyes of others. I did not want to have to share anything. I did not know what I wanted, where I wanted to be. I was screaming inside but did not know how to express my feelings. Searching for answers without even knowing the questions. Trapped in a world of fear, insecurity, guilt, feeling worthless, so very unhappy, unable to cope anymore.

After forty–eight hours I managed to find my way out of the ward, I looked so carefully around me to make sure no one was looking, I ran and ran, my heart beat so quickly. I could hear the blood pumping in my heart, I could feel my hands shaking, my back was wringing wet as I ran from the hospital grounds. Down the main road, such a long road, so much traffic, the hustle and bustle, I was so afraid but I knew inside that I had to run and run until I could find a way home.

A telephone box appeared, it did not take Glen long to come and pick me up. No anger, no recriminations, but a loving caring man who held me in his arms. He was going to take me home.

He did take me home, but first we returned to the hospital where Glen took his time to explain to the nursing team he would care for me. The case conference lasted for about two hours. Surely, you would have thought I could trust him now, but still the insecurities of the past remained with me. He took me to our flat.

I was still suffering from the effects of the medication which had been administered to me, "Largatal" a drug not used today, thank goodness. The side effects were awful, shaking, slurred speech, drooping facial features and no ability to think.

During the day my parents telephoned the hospital to see how I was and when they heard I was at the flat – they came straight round. Soon it sounded as though we had an army outside. The banging on the door was really loud. Glen was to see first hand the anger of my father, which I had so often talked about. No opportunity to reason with them, no offers of help, no understanding, nor a chance to talk. They would not listen to me. Instead my father dealt with a difficult situation in the only way he knew, with violence and aggression. He could not be reasoned with. There was nothing else to do; I called the police in order to have them evicted from the flat.

I shook from head to toe. Imagine having to call the police to your own flesh and blood. They eventually left and Glen was left to cope with me.

My parents were adamant that Glen and I would not stay together. They accused him of being the one who had led to me being ill in the first place. Not once did they see the part they had played. In the years that followed contact with them was fraught. I wanted so much to build up a relationship with them, but to be honest, I did not know how a daughter should behave to her parents. Whatever effort I made to communicate invariably broke down. Arguments were frequent.

I cannot lay the blame totally at their doorstep. I'm sure there have been times when I have probably reacted in a way which could have been wrong or taken out of proportion. I have learned to start looking at the breakdown of communication from two angles now. It does take two to put things right.

Glen and I were to be married in October 1979. Was it possible my parents would put their feelings to one side to come to see us get married? No. – Neither of them came to the wedding. Yet here we are today, twenty five years on. It can only be one thing which has seen our marriage survive, LOVE!

During the course of these events Glen introduced me to Eric Chanellor, Methodist Minister who became a very loving friend, he was so full of love and compassion for people. He was to see some of the traumatic events which were to occur. He has very kindly contributed to this story.

I feel very privileged to be able to have a part in Lynn's story. It is an amazing story of an amazing young woman. Who epitomises the subject of her book.

About six years ago I felt called to write the story of my own life in a book entitled "It So Happened, from Plough to Pulpit". The opening Acknowledgement reads "First all I want to thank God that after I accepted the challenge to write this book it so happened that three sisters were updating their computer and gave to me their old Amstrad PCWS 256 – just what I needed. Thank you Kristie, Emma and Alison Grocott"

Now their mum is writing her own story and has asked me to recall some incidents in her life in which I was involved.

My first vivid memory was having a call at midnight from a very distraught Glen. They had moved into a flat from the hospital accommodation where they had both worked. Lynn lost her job, she was disturbed and on this night had left the flat and disappeared into the darkness. The police found her and brought her back. Glen was a tower of strength.

They moved from there to a flat in Tean and it was from there that I had another call from Glen. Lynn had locked herself in her bedroom – and refused to come out. I helped to persuade her to open the door. She was so frightened and so insecure.

Glen suggested that they should get married, and asked me, if they were married in a registry office if I would be willing to conduct a Marriage Blessing service in my church at Cheadle. This we did.

Eric Chanellor, Methodist Minister

It was a very special day for both of them when their first baby daughter was born – and I had the privilege of baptising Kristie in the Methodist Church at Cheadle.

At that time I had several churches in my care, including one at Alton, close to the famous Alton Towers. It was a small church with a caretaker's cottage adjoining it. This became vacant and Glen, Lynn and Kristie moved in and Lynn helped in the Sunday school. Emma arrived and joined a happy family.

I retired in 1983 and moved to Alsager where I now live. Glen got a job in a boys' school at Denstone and they moved from Alton. He once described the family in terms of a wheel: Lynn being the hub, the girls the spokes and Glen himself the rim that bound them all together. What a wheel, and what a story!!

5: My Worst Fears

I suffered with severe mood swings, anger, fear, inability to meet people. Sometimes my emotions ran so high I would feel like a raging sea inside. I just did not know how to cope with anything any more. The only time I felt safe was when I was in Glen's company. If he and I were to go out for any length of time he used to have to imagine every single thing that may happen during that time in order for him to be able to have a coping strategy planned. He helped me to start gaining some independence slowly but surely.

Let me give you an example of how he helped me start using public transport on my own again. He encouraged me to get on a bus and while he followed the bus in the car. I would sit on the back seat so that I could see the car and know that I could get off the bus at any time and be safe.

Recovery was a long hard haul. Glen suffered so much, he was with me twenty four hours a day, trying to deal with irrationality, and knowing that at times he could not get me to see logic at all. He was, and still is, a very wise and patient man. He could see the thing that I needed most of all in my life was a baby. He knew a new meaning and purpose would start to take shape in my life. This is not the answer for everyone and I am not for one minute suggesting to those of you out there who are looking for something to help you get better, to chose having a child in your life, but it *is* what helped me.

For each individual there are certain things which can make a difference. For me I was given the chance to love someone, to care for someone, to ensure I gave my child love in the true sense of the word. To protect and nurture a tiny individual on its entry into this world.

I came under the care of Dr Shevlin, from Tean in Stoke on Trent. He is an amazing doctor who has stuck by me through many things. He tried so hard to help me in so many ways offering medication, an ear and time. He is definitely the sort of GP who really invests time into his patients.

Just to bring some humour into this story, and to let you know how human my doctor is I will tell you a funny story which illustrates how naive I was at this time. As time went on during my first pregnancy my naval started to protrude. I could not understand what was happening so Glen told me it was going to come undone. He kept telling me the same thing for weeks until I went for my antenatal check up. I plucked up the courage, “Doc, can I ask you something?”

“Yep what’s up Lynn?”

“Well it’s like this. I don’t know whether to believe him or not but Glen has told me my navel is going to come undone!”

He jumped down from the couch opened the waiting room window and shouted “Roll up, roll up! I have got the first woman here whose naval is going to come undone! Ten pence to come and see!”

I disappeared so quickly but, what a fantastic GP to have a sense of humour and to keep his humanity with his patients.

Now he sees a changed person for the first time in years and is actively involved in emails to encourage me to carry on growing and learning.

He is a doctor who believes in holistic healing, knowing how the body and mind work together and in harmony. Both need to be balanced in order for the individual to be content and happy. Balance of both leads to better health. We are no different to a plant – it is no good having healthy leaves without a healthy stem, both are needed to have a plant that shines and blooms!

Eventually our first beautiful daughter was born. She was like a miracle and helped me to cope with a lot of my pain. She gave me a new focus in life. The joy of watching the development and growth of my daughter was something I could not put into words. The first steps. Her first smile. Her first word.

It was a wonderful experience apart from the fact that she was a screaming baby and if I slept for ten full nights in the first eighteen months of her life I was lucky. Our second child was born eighteen months after the first and our third was born twenty two months after that.

What a joy those children have been. How proud I am as a mother to say that they are beautiful and are all doing really well in their lives. What treasured memories I have.

Now, the next piece of my story is something which I have hesitated as to whether I should include it or not. I do not want my children to be ashamed of their mum and I do not want to hurt them. However, I have weighed up many things and decided to share it with you in the hope it will touch some of you who may be going through something similar at this moment in time. You may be looking for a way out, for someone to tell you it can be done. Maybe you are wondering how you can do it. If you are then the answer is: if I can you can. It is you who must decide. It is you who must take the first step. It is only you who can gain self worth through believing you are as worthy as the next person.

As I have said on many occasions and will continue to say throughout this story, in order to become empowered and in control of your life, issues of the past have to be dealt with. You need to be dependent on no one. You have to believe and trust in yourself.

My past still hindered our marriage in many ways. I was still insecure. There was always a fear that Glen would leave. I tried to keep him to myself. I crushed him at times, constantly worrying whenever he wanted to go out on his own. I could not believe someone would want to stay with me. I was not worthy of their faithfulness.

Besides this I suffered with pre menstrual tension to the extent of becoming very angry each month. Sometimes I was completely out of control of my actions. For Glen it would be like treading on egg–shells. He didn't know whether he was coming or going. He tried on numerous occasions to reassure me he was not going anywhere. He loved me, he had never given me any reason to doubt him.

But my suffocating dependence tried him too hard.

When our eldest was about seven Glen met someone else. The pain, seared through me, we talked things through and I knew how much I had been to blame.

Grief was awful on the day we separated. Yes, divorce was coming my way! I had somehow got to survive, I had somehow got to still be mum to the girls. I did not know how I was going to carry on from one day to the next. It was so hard because Glen had left, he had not died but he was still alive and loving someone else!

During this time, I began to drink at night time; anything to numb the pain – to sleep. I did not want to wake up. Reality was harsh and it was cold. The girls needed my love and protection but my self worth was lower than ever. Through the mist came the drink, through the drink came the mist. Time stood still and my life had come to an end or so I thought.

I lost all self respect. There was never a day when the girls were not looked after but as for me? I just did not care. I was so reliant on Glen for love and now I hated myself so badly. With a lack of self worth my vulnerability became worse. I looked for acceptance anywhere and that *somewhere* was one of the darkest places you can imagine. I turned to drugs.

6: THE PUSHER

Not drugs from the chemist, not to those administered by my doctor, but heroin. It happened one day when I met a young lady. I had decided to try to go back into education, found a nursery for our youngest daughter and had a friend collect the other two from school. Little did I know the lady in question made her living by selling cocaine, heroin and cannabis. You name it she had it. And, it was not long before she told me how she could help me feel better – she had the answer.

Foolish and gullible, lonely and afraid I took her up on her offer.

Okay, I thought, nothing can be worse than the hell I am suffering now. Anything has got to better than reality. Let me sail through each day in a dream – please take me away from what I am facing. The first couple of fixes were free and the relief was wonderful. Floating along each day, topping it up with alcohol each night, then a sleeping tablet to end the day. This seemed like the way get through it. But not for too long though!

Soon after you're addicted and you've run out of resources to fund the drug habit, comes crunch time. Drug pushers know how to work you. They are indeed puppet masters. They get you so that you walk around with your hands held out like Oliver Twist, "More, please, more..."

I went in search of my source, palm held out for my little bit of comfort, her hand out for money in return. But I had none. Her eyes filled with a triumphant look. She'd got me where she wanted me – strings in place. Then she told me the plan. If I slept with men she would take the money and I would have my relief.

I had lost self worth, I had allowed myself to go into a world I would never have believed I would go into. But I couldn't do that. Now I had to crawl my way out.

I tried so hard to do it on my own. The stomach cramps, the shivering, the need to drink. All of that when I had three beautiful daughters, what on earth was I doing? I had to stop but how? The only answer was to register with a doctor and have help with methadone. I am glad to say my methadone programme was soon over and I was free of the need for the heroin.

I will never forget some of the people I saw as I crawled out of that pit of despair. Desperate individuals with no meaning to their lives. Lost souls searching for love, acceptance and oblivion.

I want to say at this point, to anyone who may be reading this book while travelling this dangerous path, that it is possible to live without substances. You can be happy. You can enjoy your life far more if you can actually feel, see, touch and hear, without the fog of the drugs. You see, besides stopping you from feeling the negative things in your life it is stopping you from feeling the full impact of all of the beautiful things too. And that is not living. I didn't believe life was going to be beautiful again – but I was wrong. Beauty can begin with self worth. Self worth can bring the happiness you so desire.

Then, I started to learn that I needed to change. I had to stop being so heavily dependent on Glen or anyone. I had to stop crushing him and stop doubting him. I had to start being an equal. I needed to be a wife, and look on him as a husband, a partner, and not as the father figure that I often had in the past.

Yes my longing for the true love of a father had even caused me to behave as a child in our marriage. Never once did Glen stop loving me. He still visited the children at our home and he was always there if I had something which I could not sort out myself.

During the months which followed I grew as a person, I lost some of my dependency and my relationship with Glen changed and developed into something new. I became more self–reliant which resulted in Glen feeling he wanted to come back.

I knew it was not going to be easy to trust him again, but I knew I still loved him as much as the day I had married him, but now in a different way. He had proved he still loved me because even during our time of being separated he still phoned to make sure I was all right, he did not cut me completely out of his life. If I ran into difficulty with the car he was there. I was starting to see him as an equal, a friend, someone who I could love as a partner.

There is no way I can say the return was smooth either. Doubt was at the forefront of my mind for months to come but never once did Glen give me cause to doubt him. The girls were overjoyed to have their dad come home to live. He played such a big part in their lives and they missed him so much whilst he was away. So I knew I had to give it a go. I had to give it a fresh chance to work again.

I looked at my children. I had three miracles to care for. Three individuals who myself and my husband had chosen to bring into this world. They were so precious and so vulnerable. So I focused on their childhood and I tried not to miss a moment of their development, teaching them to ride their bicycles, learning to swim, even camping out in the back garden during the summer holidays. The girls and my husband became my entire life.

7: NIGHT CARE

As the children got a little older I became a night care assistant working with the elderly. I enjoyed my job so much it was wonderful to provide care to people who needed it. I was so fortunate because the three ladies whom I worked with on a rota basis, had the same philosophy as me; to treat others as you would want to be treated yourself. The officer in charge of the home was amazing. She was a true mentor.

Now I am not saying that my way of working was the only way to work or that I deserve credit for my methods. I am trying to show that in a caring role one must have compassion and understanding. The person in residential care is vulnerable and needs to have their identity maintained. We as carers were working in *their* home, not ours. The officer in charge insisted that she did not mind if the residents' beds were not made until midday providing both the physical and emotional needs of the people in our care had been met.

But all was to change as "care in the community" was introduced and social services slowly started to close many of the homes down. Ours was one of the homes that were "surplus" to requirement and I was redeployed to another residential home.

The standard of care at this new home was so different. It was made clear that all fifty two residents had to be in bed before the night staff went on duty at ten pm and they had to be up, washed, dressed and ready for breakfast by seven forty five am. There were only two waking night staff on duty at any one time which meant in order to complete this task we had to start getting residents out of bed, washed and dressed as early as five in the morning. It meant putting some of them back into bed in their clothes. By the time breakfast was ready a vast number of them had been incontinent again but their comfort didn't seem to matter. Routine ruled over care.

It was soon made clear that I was not welcome as a member of staff within the home either. My method of working was frowned upon because it took longer to complete tasks or routine was not always possible to keep to. Routine can become ritualistic if you are not careful; you have to be flexible when it involves people, especially when dealing with a large number of people under one roof.

So, I would leave some of the residents in bed who were still asleep and I would try to make up for this by making some beds and doing other chores. I did not mind how many residents were still up and about when *I* went on duty.

It is a well–known fact as we get older that we need less sleep. Many elderly people enjoy staying up until the early hours of the morning. So why should someone who is ninety be expected to go to bed before ten o'clock at night and be expected to get up before half past seven in the morning? They had lost enough of their individuality just by coming into residential care, without impinging unnecessary restrictions on them.

During the time I worked within the home my car was vandalised on four different occasions, pots of urine were placed on the top of doors so I was drenched as I entered a resident's room. Voodoo dolls were made of me with needles protruding from them and a sleeping night duty member of staff told the officer in charge that she was so afraid of me when I was on duty that she felt the need to carry a knife to bed with her and place a chair at the back of the door of the sleep–in room.

Complaints about my work were frequently made which resulted in me being confronted by higher management just after I had finished working a ten hour night shift. I was given no warning of the meetings being arranged and no one was present from the union to witness what was said to me.

Driving into work became unbearable. I would drive the sixteen miles so slowly and as I got within two miles of the home, I would pull over to the side of the road to see how long I could delay the inevitable act of walking through the door of the home to start my night shift.

The final straw came with one poor lady who suffered with scabies. The officer in charge of the home would not declare this to the health authority in order to avoid unwanted attention. She kept the home open to day care clients and to visitors. It was not long before scabies started to spread to other residents and from them to members of staff who in turn carried it home to their families.

Going on duty one night was almost like a nightmare. Two Petri dishes and four two inch paint brushes were waiting for us. We were told to go and paint a lotion onto the residents with scabies. It sounded as though we were being asked to paint walls or garden fences. I couldn't do it. Lint and gloves were used instead. I had to leave this awful place, I was becoming ill with headaches, depression, fear and a feeling of complete worthlessness.

I am not saying life was all doom and gloom – far from it. I have said already I have the most amazing wonderful family. We enjoyed many special hours together. I had found a way to deal with my past, I repressed it I suppose, which was so easy to do when I was with my family. They compensated at least tenfold for any difficulty faced in the past.

There are so many special memories to treasure. I will give you just one example. There is a beautiful place close to us called Cannock Chase, comprising of woodland and heath. Deer can be seen grazing. My husband and I used to frequently take the girls there deer spotting at around 3 am with torch, flasks and a night vision scope. Coming home the girls would be so full of excitement, then we'd have breakfast of the most mixed variety. Sometimes they would ask if they could have chips and we would sit in the kitchen waiting them to cook, sharing stories and laughter. The smell of the heather and trees, the sound of squirrels, the sound of the girls whispering so as not to stir the wildlife. It was beautiful and amazing. How lucky I am to have memories such as these to reflect upon.

8: A Pipe Dream

As you have already heard I had a passion for Sociology. As time went on I realised how I longed to go to university. Never once had anyone seen any academic ability in me. It was Glen who brought the subject up. I began my applications and in October 1993 I was ready to start the first day of my degree in the subject. From a bad experience working in that awful residential home there had come good. From negative had come positive. Here I was on my way to university. I could hardly believe what was happening.

This was a major success in my life to be able to study a subject I was passionate about. Already I was seeing how a difficult situation could be turned around. If I had not suffered the things I had during my time working in this awful home, I would not have considered leaving social services to do what had always been a pipe dream. So with the aim of gaining qualifications to equip me to embark on a career, I was ready to enjoy the experience before me. I was also finding a way of being better equipped to apply for posts which would allow me some influence over how things were to be done.

Glen had already had to finish work due to the fact that he suffered with an illness called Guillian Barrie Syndrome. This later left him with peripheral neuropathy – nerve damage in his legs and feet. The intensity of the pain was awful and he was to find himself on high doses of morphine in order that he could manage to walk and tolerate the pain on a day to day basis. I also saw the pain in his eyes as he could no longer fulfil the role of breadwinner. I wanted so much to help and to finance our family in as many ways as possible. With this in mind I went to Derby University and enrolled. And before I knew it I was sat in my first lecture surrounded by new faces.

I remember the day Glen finally had to finish work. We were so concerned about the finances. How were we going to survive? How was I going to put food on the table? How were we going to pay the household bills?

Never once has a bill remained unpaid – something has always come up. Worrying was not the way to sort things out. Constructive action was the only way. Fear and dread did not work. Fear and dread are two very negative, destructive emotions. We all feel them, we all have them and I hope I'll help to show it is possible to channel these feelings into constructive building tools.

Then, in the first year of my degree, I found that I was suffering with pain, numbness and pins and needles in my left leg. My balance began to become unstable, at times my words would slur and I began to suffer with severe cramps and spasms in both legs. I found that trying to write cheques became impossible because I would either address them to the wrong recipient or date them wrong. Going to see a neurologist proved to be devastating. His diagnosis was multiple sclerosis (MS). The bottom was knocked out of my world. How was I going to cope? How would this impact my family?

9: Not My Dad! Not My Dad!

For those of you who do not know what multiple sclerosis is or how the nature of the illness affects the body here is a small insight into what it actually does. The brain and the spinal cord are coated with a myelin sheath. This protects the nerves. With MS the myelin sheath breaks down, exposing those nerves. As such the pathway between the messages from the brain to the nerves are affected. In turn, any part of the body can be affected, from sight, to mobility to complete debilitation. There are three types of this disease. First there's benign MS – one flare up and then back to normal. Then there's relapsing and remitting MS, where there are times when the MS is bad and then times when the sufferer feels all right. During each flare up the sufferer doesn't know which area of the body is going to be affected and whether the affected area is going to recover. Finally there is secondary progressive MS which means that the sufferer declines slowly or quickly. I have relapsing and remitting.

Within a few months of the diagnosis I was to suffer my first flare up. I became totally debilitated, unable to move, having to allow my family to wash me. The physical pain was unbelievable, to the point where it would render me into what seemed like epileptic seizures. It was my body's way of shutting down. My legs would contort with spasms and even morphine was ineffective at times. The future was so unpredictable, no one could say if I would ever get back on my feet again.

As you read further you will be given an insight into some of the challenges an MS sufferer might face. But for anyone who is reading this who has being recently diagnosed or who is caring for someone with the illness please do not think your life is over. It is most certainly not! Start straight away to look for people who can help and get as much information as you can. The main thing is that you do not live expecting the worst, or worrying about what negative impact it may have on your life. It may be unpredictable but so is life itself. Okay, a flare up may be around the corner, but then again may be it is not. So are you going to waste the precious moments of today worrying about it?

The tests used in my diagnosis included a lumbar puncture, where the spinal fluid was tapped out from the spine for analysis. An MRI scan, which is a high tech x–ray machine. I remember as they slowly moved me into it, I imagined I was going to the moon in a space rocket – anything to pass the time! There was also a test on the reaction of the eyes otherwise known as a EVP (Evoked Visual Potential) test. For those of you who like watching white dots on a television this could be quite addictive.

During a lumbar puncture, a nurse stood helping the doctor. He sat so comfortable behind me as he drew off the fluid but the poor nurse in front of me stood a little too close; a small nerve in my left leg suddenly made my leg kick out in front directly into her stomach! I felt so sorry for her, and she was obviously suffering more than me!

Six weeks passed and slowly things improved, but for how long? Not very! However, the MS was under control for the time being... It was life that delivered its next blow!

During this period I reached a point of sheer desperation. For some time my mum had been suffering with mental health problems. She could not identify where the problem stemmed from, but she became so ill that she was admitted into the local psychiatric hospital. My dad didn't know how to cope at all. He started to bring my mum to visit when he picked her up at the weekends.

I clearly remember the occasion when we were all talking and during the conversation the church and faith were bought up. Dad said that he knew that he had been forgiven for everything in his life and he knew he was going to Heaven. Here reconciliation failed as it does so often. The puppet master was cutting his strings from the puppet but me, the puppet was still attached to the tangled mess left behind.

I was still hoping for that true father and daughter bond to develop. Yes, during this time he became more mellow and my hope still persisted. However, this was not to happen.

So, there I am basically expecting the phone to ring any day with the news of my mum. I spoke to my dad on the Monday to say I had been to visit mum. I did not read between the lines because he told me the hospital were thinking of discharging her. He did not know how he was going to cope. He felt as though he had lost the woman whom he loved and could not see how he was ever going to get her back. He said, "There will be a tragedy with your mum before long." I felt sure he was right. I had to prepare myself for the fact my mum was not going to be on this earth for long.

Then the shock came on the Wednesday morning! The telephone rang with a shrill tone. My brother! What on earth was he doing on the phone? We had nothing to say or do with each other. The message was shocking! Dad had taken his own life. He had hanged himself in the shed with his dressing gown cord.

NOT MY DAD! NOT MY DAD! PLEASE! PLEASE!

10: Screams & Skeletons

Surely we were going to find time to build up a true father daughter relationship. I slid slowly down the wall – I remember the sinking feeling. All questions bubbled up inside of me. What had he done to himself? Was he dead? Had he only *tried* to take his own life? Was he bleeding? Emotions rolled from hurt, anger, fear and panic. It was like having to deal with a raging sea.

Glen took me to see my brother. We had to travel about twenty five miles. The police car was still outside. The policeman taking a statement. A photographer in the shed. I was asked if I wanted to see how dad had left the bedroom before they started to take things away from the house. I was so numb, so confused, so dazed. Surely I was going to wake up. It was like a nightmare sitting in that house because people came in and out to see my brother and they did not even realise who I was; it had been such a long time since I had last set foot in that house. The house of secrets, shame and guilt. Just another episode to add to the ones already stored in the brickwork. Also mum and dad had tried to block out the fact that they even had a daughter. Yes, you may find it hard to accept, but I was the black sheep, the daughter to be ashamed of.

The next job was to visit my mum and to break the news. Trembling and shocked I watched her tormented body walk into that room. She was living in a small annex which was attached to the psychiatric hospital. Her face was the face of an old woman with no direction and no meaning. She showed no will to survive. And here I was to tell her that the most important person in her life had died. Not only died but taken his own life and robbed her of more time with him.

She screamed...

It is a scream that I shall never forget. It was almost blood curdling. The fear on her face – a woman suddenly reduced to such a pitiful state – that it was too painful to even watch. There was such a transformation in her eyes. It was frightening, and I was the one telling her and creating all of those feelings. What was I doing? Why was I being so cruel? Surely my dad was going to wake up? Surely this was just a dream?

No dream, it was reality and now it was time to face up to that reality. No more dreaming of a father daughter relationship to be proud of. No more dreaming of a mum who would give me a hug – just cold, hard facts. He was gone. No note. No goodbye. No hug. No happy memories. Just a moment in time where he decided to leave this world and not look back.

The girls, Glen and myself, were due to go on holiday on the Saturday. Glen thought that it was right to still go and I agreed with him. There was nothing to do and hanging around was futile. So Glen spoke to my brother asking him if it was possible to have the funeral when we returned from our holiday. This was not to be.

Whilst at the hospital with my mum, my brother arranged for the undertaker to go to the house. He chose the coffin, the hymns and the funeral was arranged for two days before we came back from that family holiday. He would not postpone the funeral and so I did not attend. I just said a quiet goodbye on White Sands beach at St David's in Pembrokeshire, where I was surrounded with the love of my children and my husband.

Before going away I did visit the mortuary because I knew that I would not be welcome at the Chapel of Rest. I had to just make sure that he really *had* gone. He lay there looking so peaceful. My initial thoughts were that he was asleep, but as I touched his shoulder, I realised that he was as cold as ice. I thought about how his heart had been as cold as his body was now.

But despite what he'd done, he should not have died on his own. No one ever should. I still wonder what went through his mind as he walked down the stairs, up to the shed. What was he feeling as he put the noose around his neck? What did he think in his final moments? I cannot work out whether the actual act was selfish or took guts – real guts. I hope dear reader that you can somehow visualise how lonely this particular moment must have been. As I write and share this with you I can feel a sense of emptiness and desperation. Not for me but for anyone who feels they must make the choice of death over life.

I think of what my dad has missed out on. He had three beautiful granddaughters and should have been as proud as a peacock, but he robbed himself of a life which could have been full of golden moments. I often wonder, what if during those final seconds, he wanted to live. How I think back to this day, wondering even now if there was more I could have done?

I did not realise just how much of a hold the repressed memories of my childhood had upon me. They had not been dealt with. I had not really overcome the abuse suffered as a child. I was still a victim. Night time became horrific. I would doze off to sleep but I woke so often in the night in sheer and utter panic. I would see a distinct and very real image in the room. It was of my dad hanging from a rope. I could see the rope spinning and spinning. His body went round and round. The shoes were like those of a dancer but when I looked up I could not see his face. I could smell a vile stench of breath which was also very hot. I could hear breathing and panting but no face.

These visions were to become more and more pronounced each and every night. At times the image would come closer and closer towards the bed, a skeletal hand would appear holding a knife and the knife would stab out towards me. It was so vivid, so real, I would try to move further and further away from the image but it followed me. The puppet master haunted me but now only I could sever the strings.

Once again the puppet master had severed his strings from me but had not given me the chance to unravel the mess of my strings. He was holding me back. Just as I thought I was free I would be snapped straight back to reality. It is a bit like a bungee jumper, freedom to fly and dive, but the elastic only goes so far. The pull comes and you are suddenly jolted back – once again confined and restricted.

11: ROOTLESS

Maybe I thought the end of tragedy had come. It was not to be. Mum continued to be very ill. She moved from hospital into residential accommodation. She became unrecognisable. Medication caused her to pile weight onto what was once a frail body and she lost any desire to change into the lovely clothes she owned.

The shrill sound of the phone again. This time my aunt called.

Mum had suffocated herself with a plastic bag in the early hours of the morning. Not one parent, but two in such a short space of time. This had definitely got to be a horrible nightmare! Not the case. She had gone and that was it. I had to find a way of coming to terms with it. Again, I had no chance to say goodbye face to face. No chance of a hug or to tell each other we really cared.

I asked to be a part of the funeral arrangements but once again this was not to happen. However, this time I *did* attend the funeral. I felt like a stranger. I had my own beautiful family who loved me so much but I had a sense of rootlessness.

You may be wondering why I found myself grieving when I had suffered the things I had. It's easy, your mum and dad are still your mum and dad no matter what.

It's strange but I always believed I would not feel any sadness or miss them. But how wrong I was. I began to ask so many questions in my own mind. I longed for one more day to see each of them and to hear their voices. Why hadn't I put things right between us? Why had I not told mum that I *did* love her in my own way? Too late for regrets though. I just hope that this will speak to your hearts and make you think about mending any broken relationships in your life.

I slowly began to realise that I was never going to know why my parents had decided to leave this earth, but it was no use in allowing them to stop me from living each day. I had to move on, not only for my sake, but for those around me.

You can always carry memories of people or situations in your heart and you have the ability to draw on those memories when you choose to, learning to make them good memories, ones which make you feel warm or loved. You can access them or learn to leave them for when it is appropriate to use them.

During this time the MS had been all right to cope with; it was more of a hindrance than anything. The first flare up was bad but it was over now. I had a limp, but that was not too much to cope with. In fact I had some amusing moments!

Going into the supermarket one day I did something that we as children always imagine would be so much fun. My balance was a little bit off and I didn't feel quite myself... then I lost my balance, I could hear two of my girls chuckling in the background. "There she goes again", they thought as my body got closer to the ground. But the stack of cola bottles was just too close. Contact was unavoidable. The bottles fell one after the other rolling down the aisle. I smiled inside, "Wow", I thought, "I have done what I always dreamt of doing!"

The girls pulled me to my feet, "You must take more water with it!" said one. "Yes " said the other, " we wish you would not drink in the morning." An old lady close by heard all of the commotion and she couldn't wait to catch up with her friend to tell her about the drunken mother in charge of two children who had just demolished the store.

12: Smell The Roses

I graduated from my degree with a 2.2 and then it happened!

MS was to start rearing its ugly head again. Turning from a hindrance into something which was going to have a dramatic impact on my life and those who loved me. I was soon to find that I was bedridden for about four weeks out of every six. Once again I was reliant on my family to take care of every need. I found myself being catheterised and needing frequent enemas. The bedroom soon started to look like a hospital room with commodes, wheelchairs and tracking hoists. District nurses were coming in and eventually social services drew up a care plan in order for regular care assistants to come into the home to help with washing, bathing and many other physical needs.

The hurt soon started to show on the faces of my children and my husband. I often used to say that it is harder for a loved one to watch their partner suffer than for the person who is physically suffering. This proved to be true. But not once did my family stop loving me and believing in my spirit to survive. Their patience and their love was amazing; three young girls learned how to care for their mother while allowing her to maintain dignity.

I was in and out of hospital on a frequent basis, whilst attempts were being made to find the right combination of drugs to allow me some quality of life. Our eldest daughter would even come to the hospital to ensure I got a bath each day. My husband never faulted in his compassion and his care. He had to spoon feed me when every single part of me refused to work.

My jaw began to spasm with the MS to such an extent it was impossible to get any medication into my mouth. Botox injections were administered into the muscles. Amongst many other uses Botox is designed to freeze and paralyse the facial muscles in an attempt to stop the clamping. Each set of injections were supposed to last for twelve weeks, however, the effect of regular top ups reduced the efficiency bringing the time span down to just eight weeks of relief.

I used to try to make a joke of things calling it the pickled onion test. You see, I could tell how things were deteriorating when I could no longer get a pickled onion in my mouth. I am talking of the small silver skin ones by the way, not the huge ones! I know I have a reputation for talking but that's just daft!

Eventually I was sent to see an oral surgeon who decided to operate in order to sever some of the muscles and nerves. There never goes a week when I do not think of this compassionate surgeon, Mr Perry. I went in to surgery with a mouth that would only open three centimetres wide and came out with thirteen whole centimetres of opening power. I think my husband sometimes wishes the surgeon had devoiced me while I was under the knife – as life would have been very much more peaceful for him!

At this point in time it seems appropriate to include some of the records of a journal which Glen kept of the repeated flare ups.

26/05/01

Flare up lasted twenty six days.

During this time, Lynn lost mobility and due to an inability to stand or balance an indwelling catheter was fitted. Left arm and leg affected with total loss of mobility on and off. Double vision, slurred speech and problems putting thoughts into words. Most difficult thing to cope with was the amount of pain she was in for the whole period of this. Her jaw was totally clamped down. Liquid food only.

30/07/01 – 27/08/01 (34 days since last flare up)

Extremely tight band around chest. Pain down spine. Severe leg spasms from thighs to ankles causing toes to be drawn back. Loss of mobility. Catheter needed. Jaw in spasm. To give her any physical help i.e. to sit up in bed or to move from bed to commode causes Lynn a great deal of pain and to me causes the same in emotional pain.

Many other flare–ups happened which Glen documented – this was written on 24th April 2002...

Lynn is in so much pain from back and legs that she has told me if I should find her in an overdose situation I should not do anything which would bring about a revival. I have agreed. She has told her friend Viv the same.

19/05/02

Lynn has had three falls, last one at six pm. Followed by six fits. Ambulance called. Oxygen given. Rectal diazepam given.

20/05/02

Catheter fitted with difficulty brought on more fits.

18/08/02

Lynn went into a coma like state. Right side of mouth drooping, as if in a stroke. Body was so still. No response to audio stimulation, or pain stimulation. Breathing gasping from time to time. Lasted twenty minutes. Both legs rigid.

I hope the above gives you some idea of what my family had to watch unable to do anything but care.

It was strange lying in bed for weeks on end, the minutes drifted into hours, then into days. Sometimes I would sleep through exhaustion, at other times I would sleep through the amount of medication. The pain consultant explained at times that I was taking enough morphine to give myself a general anaesthetic. During the waking times the pain would come in waves. I would get cramps in my legs so severe that it felt as though my tendons were being ripped and torn in shreds. Sensory disturbances in both arms and legs felt, and still do feel at times, as though rats are biting at the nerve endings.

But not once did I lose sight of the fact that my children and Glen loved me. Happy memories looked down on me all the time from photographs on the walls; pictures taken by Glen of our holidays in Wales. A picture board created by Alison, of childhood memories, it still hangs on the wall today. How my heart smiles when I think of the way in which she lovingly put it together.

The smell of flowers always filled the room. Glen grew roses, all with a fragrance. I did not have the strength to sit outside so he brought the garden inside for me. Audio tapes were bought for me to listen to as watching the television required too much concentration.

When I was well enough to sit outside, Glen loving devoted his time to creating a beautiful garden. I was so impressed with his kindness and compassion the following article went into the newspaper. It was done to show carers that it is possible to ease the suffering of the one being cared for by just thinking of things to bring peace to them.

"GROCOTT, WHAT HAVE YOU DONE NOW, YOU LUNATIC?"

by Nermin Oom

"That was the first thing Glen said to me when he found out I had called the paper to tell you about him with our garden" giggles Lynn.

"With all the bad happening in the world I thought it would be nice for people to hear about something good."

"I want to publicly thank Glen for caring for me for all these years and to show people that despite attending to my every need, he still can create something as beautiful as our garden which brings me so much joy. I love to hear people commenting on the roses."

"He puts so much thought and effort into making sure I can enjoy the garden even if I'm unable to move around. It's a labour of love."

Lynn 43, and Glen 54 have been married for over 23 years. The couple met through work. Ten years ago Lynn was diagnosed with multiple sclerosis. She has good days and bad days where she is paralysed, meaning she is totally dependent on Glen.

"The disease is so unpredictable", says Lynn. "It means we can never plan anything as I can never tell how I'm going to wake up."

She loves to be outside watching the wildlife scurry by, listening to the sounds of running water and taking in the smells of the flowers.

"I wanted to create a refuge, a place of tranquillity and calm for Lynn," says softly spoken Glen." Every flower in this garden has a scent, there's a wildlife pond, a pond with ornamental fish and a rose garden. We can light up the garden at night or in the winter so she can still see it from the house. Lynn doesn't have to be able to move around to enjoy it. Its her sanctuary when all hell is breaking lose in her body"

I have to agree it certainly is a peaceful place with a calming influence. No two corners are the same and on closer inspection, it's full of surprises. There are pot fairies hiding behind the bushes, a stone lion keeping his eye on the insects flitting around the pond.

Lynn confirms it brings her great pleasure. "It's the next best thing to being by the sea."

I fought my way from flare up after flare up and each time I won. It was so hard. Emotions ran wild in my mind. I went through anger, anger at the world, anger at

God. I went through "Why me?" I went through denial. When I was feeling a bit better I would rush around, burning myself out, trying so hard to catch up for lost time. I could not let myself waste one second. Sometimes I would go to bed feeling a little bit under the weather and I would think, "Please not another flare up!"

13: MAYBE...

Then the grieving came. Yes with disability people can grieve for the part of them that used to work so well. You lose something you once took for granted, it has gone and how you miss it. For example, using a hand. You may be so used to do things with that hand. One day it is gone and you are left having to train yourself to be without it.

Then came the self pity. I was forced to stop driving; my co–ordination and my perception had changed so much that I was not safe to be behind the wheel of a car. I found it so hard to come to terms with my loss of freedom, my ability to jump in the car and take myself off. Independence had been reduced again. I was trapped – reliant on others to take me out. Living in a rural community, your own transport is invaluable, public transport is so limiting. My wheels had been taken from under me.

I had always believed I would not land up in a wheelchair for any length of time but how wrong I was. I found myself wheelchair bound on many occasions usually lasting a couple of weeks. Then came the big one, not weeks but months of using a chair. No more walks up at Cannock Chase, no freedom to roam around the shops, dependent on people to get from A to B around the house. No upper body strength to be able to propel myself either.

Then I found a group of people had started a fund raising campaign for me. They raised enough money for a motorised wheelchair and also purchased the very computer I am writing this story on. What wonderful people!

I thought long and hard about the teaching of sociology and its theory on language. I suddenly started to realise the importance of how we word things.

I will never get out of this wheelchair...

I may be able to get out of this wheelchair...

I will never get out of the wheelchair and I will never have any life...

I may get out of this wheelchair, but even if I don't I can still lead an enjoyable life...

That was it language! How we speak and how we think is all based on our everyday thoughts. Our conscious actions influenced by our subconscious. If I told myself I could possibly get out of this wheelchair maybe I could. Anything was worth a try.

Can you see the difference the words make when you read them? There is hope in the "maybe able." It changes the way people think. With this in mind I started to change my whole way of looking at MS.

I was determined I was going to fight my way out of the chair. I wanted so much to stand again. I owe so much to my physiotherapist, Nicola White, who came on domiciliary visits each Friday. She worked so hard with me. I asked her to set unrealistic goals and she was fantastic. She showed delight on her face as she entered the door each week and found I had achieved the goals she had set. Her words were always to take things at a steady pace, to listen to my body. I did this but equally I knew I had to push myself.

The pain of taking a few steps was immense, the muscle wastage meant my legs would buckle so easily and I frequently lost my balance. However, with time, persistence and support my legs slowly got stronger and I was able to take more steps. The sense of achievement was wonderful, however the pain still persisted. Various drugs were tried but to no avail. I was admitted into hospital for a period of five weeks in an attempt to find some medication to try to bring some form of relief from the symptoms.

Many events took place during this time. I was taken for an MRI scan to see if there was any deterioration of the myelin sheath. I had been in so much pain that I took an extra tablet on the morning of the scan and was given some diazepam to help to keep me calm whilst the scan took place.

I will never forget that day. I woke up to find a team of doctors around me and a resuscitation machine. My tee shirt was cut straight up the middle. I had lost consciousness. My blood pressure was all over the place and I just could not wake up.

I owe so much to my neurological consultant, Dr Simon Ellis, who has stood by me with compassion. He has fought for me and been willing to try almost anything to ease the symptoms. He is a consultant who has never lost his compassion for people, never once has he looked at me in any other way than as a person – not just another patient. Thank you so much Dr Ellis.

While there, my consultant asked me if I would be willing to see if a psychiatrist could help me to find ways to mentally cope with the pain I was going through. I agreed.

The mind and body are interconnected and physical pain can and does have a mental impact. Especially long–term pain. It can make you feel low at times and I knew, deep down inside, if I could find a way of mentally dealing with the physical pain I could deal with any disability.

It takes time to get used to not being able to use a leg or an arm but it *is* possible. Pain is debilitating in the true sense of the word. Let's face it – the pain was keeping me from getting out of bed during a flare up. It was causing me to have to use excessive medication just to sleep. I was missing out on time and time as we all know is precious.

14: Mauled, Chewed At, Torn

During the course of my sessions with the psychiatrist, my family background got delved into. The sessions lasted for about three quarters of an hour once per month.

This form of treatment was devastating. I am not blaming the psychiatrist for this but there are so many resources needed to handle people who are suffering emotionally. To some extent emotional suffering is worse than any physical pain. You see, if someone has a broken leg people can see where it hurts, but with emotions it is difficult to explain and often the emotions are irrational. Therefore the psychiatrist is trying to deal with illogic from the stand–point of logic.

Each counselling session resulted in a fit. These fits were labelled "dissociative state fits" brought on because the emotional pain was too great to face the situation being talked about.

So many wounds were opened up and I was then left to go back home and to deal with all the emotions the sessions had brought back out. When I use the words wounds, it was as though I was bleeding inside, cut, mauled, chewed at, torn apart. It was indescribable. I felt at times as though I was climbing the walls, going mad. The nightmares were horrific. I was afraid of even shutting my eyes. The physical and emotional abuse of my childhood became so real and vivid again that at times I was reliving it.

I kept having the same dreams over and over. One that I vividly remember is of driving down the street in which I grew up. Each of the doors in the road would open as I passed them in the car, and a skeleton would be thrown out by the families living in each house. I would not even wake up until Glen shook me awake but then I would remain locked in my nightmare. The room would be full of skeletons, Glen would resemble my dad and minutes, which seemed like hours, would pass before I realised I was safe. Cold sweat would be pouring down my face and my hands would be clenched along with my teeth, so scared, so lost, I could not see an end.

The initial images during the night returned, not one night was going by without me waking up to the twirling body from the rope. I couldn't eat. I felt dirty. I was scared. I hated the dark. The darkness allowed *him* to appear. He came from nowhere, lurking in the darkest corner, sometimes so close to the bed he was within an inch of touching me. My life was becoming one long nightmare, praying for light, dreading the dark, once again dreading climbing into bed. My abuser was still in my life. I was allowing him to control me. Still the puppet, I was being manipulated.

My family were the only ones supporting me. They suffered immensely.

Our daughters went through some horrendous times and one of them became really poorly but that remains her story to tell. However, what I will say is that this too had a vast impact on our family. I was told I was suffering with post traumatic stress.

One session, in particular, with the psychiatrist is etched on my memory. We talked openly about the death of my father and how he had gone without leaving any letter – no goodbye. I found myself almost in a trance like state; I could hear his voice, feel the pounding of his fists, just as I had done when I was a little girl. I could feel his hands over my body. I could smell his breath, see the whites of his eyes, so close, we were face to face now. I'd lost touch with reality and it was too much. My mind shut off.

I woke up having been incontinent on the floor of the consulting room. But I was not in the consulting room in my mind; I was in my parental home, the puppet master was there, he was alive, then he was hanging and my mother was laughing, screeching like a witch. People were shouting in the background but my attention could not be moved from the images around me. Eventually the nightmare faded. The psychiatrist, a paramedic, a doctor and three other members of staff were all focused on me. They wanted me to agree to be admitted onto the acute ward of the psychiatric hospital.

They telephoned Glen who reassured them this was *not* the right place for me to be. There would be too many memories of where my mum had been. So I was allowed home into the safe hands of my family. The following days were spent living in fear, dreading the return of these waking nightmares.

It was at this time I decided to phone Tony Burgess. I knew him because he taught two of my daughter's. But besides teaching, I had also heard of his reputation as a counsellor. There was not the slightest hesitation in his voice. He wanted to help and he offered to come to the house to see me.

15: A Day In The Life of An Anorexic

By the time Tony and I met, I had started to suffer with anorexia. My initial weight was eight stones and two pounds. I could not bring myself to eat because I had started to feel so big, fat, ugly and worthless. I had lost about a stone when I first saw him. The kitchen cupboards started to look deformed, the contents inside seemed huge and out of perspective. Panic would set in if anyone mentioned me eating. I had started to resort to weighing myself about five times each day. I started to abuse laxatives, because I felt like I needed cleansing from the inside out.

The lack of eating became a form of control. I was in control of what products went inside me. I was in control of my body. I was in control of my weight. I was not being force fed sweets and then being made to compromise myself.

But what I did not see was that I was *out* of control because of the hold that this illness now had upon me. I wanted to become insignificant. I suppose I thought that by becoming smaller no one could hurt me because I could blend into the background. I wanted to become almost like a child again in size. I despised my body. I felt worthless and undeserving of food and nutrition. I also felt unclean and at times would take up to four baths each day. I felt violated. I relived the abuse so vividly that it was like being raped all over again.

Let me give you an account of a typical day in the life of an anorexic.

On waking up, your bones hurt where they have been pressing on the mattress, hips are raw, shoulder bones ache, legs feel like jelly. That's before you have even got out of bed. You are tired because you have drifted in and out of sleep, both from hunger and the fact that too few calories have been consumed to allow sleep to come. Yes, we even need calories to be able to sleep properly.

Head aching, through lack of nutrition and a dry mouth. Fingers trace the outline of your body. Has any bone been covered with more flesh during the night? Right hand must be placed around the left wrist to see if the little finger and the thumb meet, not only meet, but, allow the digits to overlap.

You look at the clock, this is a moment when you could allow yourself to drift back into sleep for a moment, thinking today, "I may feel differently." Then your mind races to tasks ahead. People in the house will need *feeding*. *Food* will have to be smelled, prepared and cooked. It seems one long haul of food, food, food! Even the dog needs to be fed.

You sit up, taking a moment to allow the room to stop spinning, then, swing your legs out of bed, standing takes so much effort, but it has got to be done. How does the stomach feel today? Is it any bigger than yesterday, or does it feel flat and tight? What about the legs, especially the thighs, are they any bigger? Go to the bathroom – all urine must be passed because the main task of the morning has got to be done... the weigh–in.

All urine passed, you undress and even take off your bracelet; it may add an ounce to the weight staring at you from the scales. Panic now sets in, what if you have gained an ounce since yesterday? How will you get through the day? Adrenaline pumps through your veins, your heart races and you clean your teeth instead. That is enough to delay the deed which has become so much a part of your routine. You are controlled by the pull of the scales, the reading on them – just another puppet master.

Your feet move closer to the inevitable action. But what if someone has messed with them during the night? How will you know they are reading right? You step out with fear and trepidation, time to do it! Go on, go for it, one foot on, then the other, stand tall. Afraid to look down now! You take a deep breath, heart pounding now as if it is going to burst out of your chest, looking down you see with relief the scales read the same as yesterday!

But are the scales right? How can you be sure? No guarantees! Try on the jeans that fitted yesterday. They feel the same so today is not going to be too bad, until people start asking what you have eaten for breakfast. Not to worry though, you can get out of that one. The answer is easy; you do everyone a drink then dive into the household chores then they will easily forget to ask.

Into the kitchen, reach for the laxatives, you hope and pray you are going to go to the toilet in a minute, if not how are going to be able to drink anything? Maybe if you have a hot drink it will help get things moving. Yes, success. The stomach cramps are bad today causing you to feel sick, but you don't care. At least you know the laxatives are working. Ah, stomach empty, feeling relieved you swing into action. Nervous energy starts to release itself and you cannot sit down because you have got to burn the calories off.

As you go about the daily chores, your knees often buckle. You sit and stand with caution, never too quickly in case you faint. It is sometimes frightening because as you stand your heart races through lack of nutrition. Where is the energy coming from?

You look in the mirror, an obese body stares back at you. Ugliness, *greed*, how can you lose more weight? Easy, use more laxatives. Not long before the evening dose. Muscles ache now and skin feels tight. Time for a soak in the bath, taking off your clothing you check yourself in the mirror again. Can you see the bones? Yes, but they are not sticking out enough. You could still get thinner – you still weigh too much. Maybe if you had not eaten that biscuit yesterday. There was no need to eat it – you were just being greedy. How dare you feed this unworthy body? How could you?

Then a flashback. Back in your cot where your father deprived you of water because you were being greedy. You had to learn to be more patient. You weren't hungry – just greedy. If you made yourself wait for a little while longer the hunger would pass, just as the thirst had passed on the night you were crying for water. And so you lie down and go to sleep knowing for a short while you will have a short time of peace during the time your body closes down.

Peace descends but not for long, your mind still active, obviously still in turmoil, as you dream of food! Sometimes the dream involves being force fed. Sometimes food seems to surround you, coming from every direction. You are tempted and your mouth opens, teeth bite into perhaps a cake, then you wake with a start – sweat on your brow. Thank goodness the dream is over.

You get up yet again. Your head swims, legs feel weak, still lots to do. How are you going to get through the day? Back on the scales, an ounce has crept on because you drank earlier. You know logically it is always best to weigh yourself in the morning, but it does not stop the fear, the panic, the racing heart.

Thirst now sets in. Your mouth is hot. Ice cubes will help cool the feeling down and crunching on them will ease the acid building up inside your stomach. Off to the freezer. Suck them slowly... but the temptation is too much. You bite into them, savouring every crunch. Food and drink all in one cube. The satisfaction of being able to use the muscles of the jaw is wonderful. How fantastic to be biting on something solid. Now make sure the ice cube tray is full with water again. Into the freezer it goes, ready for later.

The day goes on and on. Exhausted, you pray for rest. You take more laxatives at night time. One more than usual tonight because the effect is wearing off. You give no consideration to the effect all of this is having on your kidneys. You do not even think about the strain you are putting on your heart muscles as they go into overdrive trying to provide your muscles with blood and oxygen. You are trapped in the hall of mirrors. You do not even give consideration to the fact you are in self–destruct mode. You do not even consider the effect you are having on your family. Your puppet master this time is the scales.

There were nights when I could not even sleep in our bedroom. I was afraid of the dark, as the lights went off images would start to gather around me. Feelings of panic, claustrophobia and heart racing terror, would roll into one. I had to get out of the room. It resulted in endless nights wandering around the house and watching television. Anything to fill the dark hours.

I slept in the day because I was so tired.

Enough was enough. It was time to sort this out once and for all. The past wasn't behind me where it should be – it right in front of me.

So that was the me – a frightened shadow, suffering with anorexia, still haunted by my childhood, still being haunted by the suicide of two parents.

Yes I had come to terms with the fact I had MS but at times it still rendered me into fits of despair. I still did not value myself. I was not happy with the person I was. I was still searching and striving for happiness.

16: An Experiment

Tony came to our house one Tuesday evening and spent about two hours with me. I immediately felt comfortable with him. He was not going to judge me and it was so easy to open up to him. I was right. Not once during the conversation did he show any sign of rejection in his voice. He listened in a way that I have not known anyone listen before, apart from of course, my husband.

But Glen was too closely involved and it was so difficult for me to accept what he was saying. I knew he loved me – he was so frustrated because there was nothing he could do other than keep reassuring me of his love and he was so tired with everything he had suffered through my illness.

I don't think there was anything Tony did not pick up on. Even my body language was observed. He had obviously heard things through our conversation I had not even said out loud and instantly he knew how he could use these points to help in my healing process. Not once did he impose any decisions on me, but he asked me how *I* would change things.

Towards the end of this first meeting Tony asked me to allow him to try out a small experiment with me. I agreed and he started to teach me the art and value of visualisation.

This is the point where I can honestly show you how victims can become winners. Also how adversity and challenge can be overcome. How negativity can be turned into positivity and life can become worth living again. What's more, life can become better than it has *ever* been because you can gain control. You can find yourself growing and suddenly longing for new challenges because you get to choose.

Before going into the detail of Tony's experiment, I would like to share with you an analogy. Once again I cannot take the credit for this but owe the wisdom to my fantastic husband.

If one takes a photograph with a camera then a negative is formed. It has to be developed in the dark. Then out of the negative comes a beautiful colour photograph. This can be applied to the hard unwanted challenges in our lives (the negatives). Out of these we can grow. We can become more understanding human beings. We can find beauty. We can learn that all challenges and setbacks contain a gift – if you look for it.

Tony asked me to close my eyes. I was asked to relax and slowly imagine there was a large cinema screen in front of me. I was able to adjust the volume of the sound and also the speed of the scenes being played. I was then to imagine looking at the screen showing the young Lynn being abused by her father. It was such a powerful exercise, at first it was too painful to look but with time and a gentle voice Tony gently reassured me that all would be all right.

As I became easier in my mind knowing that I could escape from the images, I was asked to change all the colours in my mind, to speed up the events, slow them down and to eventually imagine going into the screen and rescuing the young Lynn, holding her in my arms and telling her that all that had happened was not her fault.

I will never forget the first time I did this. It was horrific to watch and see what had happened when I was so small. I had been blaming myself for years and now I suddenly saw that as a child I was a blameless victim. I could not have stopped the man who called himself my dad from doing what he did. My heart went out to the young Lynn in the picture. I wanted to hold her forever and to tell her she was safe. This was not the end of the guilt by any means but it was a start. I began to see how my father was unstoppable at that time. I had been too young to do anything to prevent what had happened. I was blameless.

We practised this exercise for several minutes. Then Tony introduced me to a new tool called an anchor. He taught me that if I needed to bring this image to mind, and reinforce it for a while, I could do it more efficiently by finger squeezing. The harder I squeezed my fingers the easier it became to perform this exercise and to bring it to mind quickly.

So when feelings of guilt and shame started to creep in, I was now able to slowly bring the screen to mind and rescue the young Lynn from her torment. This kind of visualisation seems so simple and obvious – and you may be thinking I'm trying to sell you on some miracle cure – but I'm not. What I am saying to you is that visualisation has become an important part of my life and it is a tool that has produced fantastic, positive changes for me.

The ability to use it effectively did not come instantly, but the more you use it, the easier it becomes to access it. And the easier it is to access to access the more powerful it becomes. The beauty of this amazing and wonderful tool is that people can play with it to suit themselves. It is about allowing your mind to be creative and to build on images that allow peace and acceptance to enter your life.

There are still issues today that I struggle with but this one thing did so much good in itself and I know that by accessing my toolbox I will overcome them too.

So, if you who are curious about how to access the tool of visualisation I will attempt to give you a small insight into the simplicity of it.

I would like you to try an experiment.

Go into a quiet room and close your eyes. Then think of a time or a place where you have been totally happy and at peace. It may be a holiday or a time where you have been for a memorable walk; anything that has made you feel good. When you have the picture in your mind, imagine how you felt at that moment. As you take your time to keep this picture in mind start to imagine the sounds that you heard and the tastes and smells you experienced. Can you feel the emotions you experienced too? Now open your eyes if you like and think how good it would feel if you could access those emotions any time you wanted. With practice this is possible too.

During the days to follow my first meeting with Tony there were horrendous times too. Times when I really felt that I would never get any sort of life back. I felt like I was going to be mentally tormented for the rest of my life.

The girls and Glen were so solid in their support, I cannot tell you how much they went through and at times I am sure they felt we would never get to the end of suffering.

However, Tony was as good as his word. He said that he would help me in whatever way he could. He was always available at the end of the phone – he emailed me. Nothing was too much trouble.

Tony gave me his time, and as my husband says, "You can't give anyone anything more important than time."

You think of a little child who asks for a mother's time, the mother says, "in a minute", or "when I've finished this." To the child the minute seems like an eternity and the moment of importance has passed.

But if I needed Tony he knew that I needed him *then* and there. This was so different to anything I had experienced with the counselling at the hospital; I knew I didn't have to see a crisis through on my own.

The other vital thing Tony promised was complete honesty and he never once promised anything unless he knew that he could fulfil his word. It was by seeing his commitment that I was able to develop a sincere trust in him. And in doing this I began a journey that has taken me to where I am today.

Insecurity, lack of self worth and guilt were so intense in my life. I could not accept I had any value.

"I have nothing to offer anyone", was a sentence which flowed so naturally from my lips. So deeply embedded in my mind, body and soul. I spent hours testing the love of my family in many ways. Sometimes by picking an argument for no apparent reason. Sometimes my over sensitivity would lead me to feel criticised when people were just having a bit of fun.

17: LIFE IS LIKE A BOX OF FROGS

Then out of blue Tony hit on something I had succeeded in doing. He began to make me feel proud of an area in my life. I, with the help of my husband, had successfully turned sexual and physical abuse around to create a loving family. My daughters were wonderful. They had known nothing but love and respect. They had seen their mum ill and had supported me, but not once had they ever been told they weren't loved or valued. They knew the meaning of a proper cuddle from parents. Then I started to look at some of the ways in which this had been achieved.

Time was the main factor. They had always had my time. If one of them wanted anything then everything I was doing at the time stopped for them in an instant. We spent endless hours playing games, having mother and daughter nights where we would drag sleeping bags down from upstairs, and spend the night sleeping in the living room. Every Saturday night became party night. We would leave Glen watching whatever he wanted to on television and we would go into the biggest bedroom in the house, watch videos or play games, and have party food. Each weekend day was devoted to their wishes; be it cycling or going shopping, to the cinema or for walks. Slowly I started to see what a fantastic achievement this was. My children knew the value of true parental love!

Tony gave me a book to read called *Feel the Fear and Do it Anyway*. It has had a remarkable impact on my life. I realised to conquer anything in life, there was always going to be an element of fear. But if we learn to face up to fear we do have the resources and the strength to overcome fear and to gain strength and insight from it.

Through reading the book I began to realise that sometimes we need to step out of our comfort zone.

A comfort zone is something or somewhere where we feel at ease. An obvious example here is where a woman may feel uncomfortable entering a pub on her own. If she does it anyway then she has stepped out of her comfort zone. I was soon to learn how to step out of comfort zones on a regular basis.

How many people suffer with a true phobia? It's a difficult thing to explain to someone who doesn't share it, isn't it? One of the most common phobias is that of spiders but for me there was another thing.

There was one thing I knew I needed to exert some control over. I had a phobia of frogs. Such a minor thing, I can hear you thinking but they terrified me.

How I loved summer days sat outside, playing with the girls, looking at the garden that Glen had lovingly created. But there was one thing spoiling the joy and peace! Glen had built a fish pond in the garden and frogs like water. No matter how secure your garden is, if you have got a pond frogs will find a way in!

The only way I can explain to you how a frog looked to me was by its size. Surely they were at least 30 centimetres – a foot in length. When they hopped they launched – surely high enough to clear a fence! I know if you have a phobia that you will be able to relate to this.

It was raining one morning, in early spring. I went outside to fill the coal bucket and there it was, the king of all frogs! I am sure he looked right at me. I ran for cover, coal going everywhere. I grabbed Kristy and Emma and locked them outside refusing to let them in until that frog had gone! The feelings of panic and anxiety were all–consuming. My blood racing and my heart was pounding. I really felt sick.

Right I thought, this is not funny any more. This fear of frogs has got to be dealt with. I told Glen I wanted to get over my phobia and without any doubt in his eyes he said he would help.

The day came when he found a baby frog. It was now or never! He was so patient holding it just as close as I could deal with. Slowly but surely with the knowledge that Glen would not let any harm come to me I reached out a trembling hand. The baby hopped onto my hand. No – I wouldn't leap a mile – I was going to conquer this phobia which had been with me since I was eight years old!

I managed to remain calm and then I was elated, laughing, jumping for joy. Now, I wait for the frogs to come out when it is raining. No longer afraid. They are beautiful creatures.

Life is indeed a box of frogs, you face challenges all the time and sometimes you'll be afraid. But it is how we deal with them that matters. Do we face those challenges head on, with courage, or do we hide away, allowing circumstances to be beat us. Life has so much good to offer that hiding away from it is a true tragedy. It is a certain fact that we cannot jump over *all* the obstacles in our life. We sometimes can't go round them or under them. There are times when we have got to go through them with the knowledge that when we come out the other side those old fears can never stop us again.

There were so many issues to deal with during my three years of working with Tony that it is difficult to recount them all. The main thing I learned was no matter what life throws in our direction we have a choice. Do we reach down into our inner most being and find the strength to deal with issues that test our resourcefulness or do we choose to be a victim? Do we allow circumstances to rule us, to pull our strings as if we were puppets or do we find a way of breaking free? A way to maintain control of how we feel?

I was so sick and tired of being tied to the past because it was hindering my relationship with my husband and my children. It was causing me to become a hermit. I used to feel so sorry for myself because I was not getting out and meeting people. Life surely had more to offer. Where was the Lynn who used to smile and be so full of life?

The healing process for me could be likened to going on a journey. Sometimes it was exciting and sometimes frightening. I want you to try to imagine a ship out at sea, on an adventure. At times the waves are calm, the sun shines, the direction is clear but at other times mist creeps in, the sky turns black with gales and waves so high the boat is tossed around from one course to another. At times like this, the strength and determination of the captain is so important. The knowledge that shore can eventually be reached is etched on the captain's mind. He knows he has many resources needed to pull the ship out of peril. And in using these resources and remaining flexible he learns new techniques which he carries with him. Then if ever the same crisis appears again, he has more resources to deal with the same situation more effectively in the future.

I found on my journey that there were times when I would reach small goals and feel so pleased. Another part of the past in its place, another string severed, a stronger more resilient Lynn emerging. Then there were big obstacles. I used to look at them, feeling vulnerable, afraid, not knowing where the next bit of energy would come from. It was during this time that Tony taught me coping skills and made me feel I had so much to offer.

The start of Lynn growing was a slow painful time. But now I am starting to bloom and feel so different.

18: In Control

Smoking had been something I felt strongly about. For me it was not right, but somehow I was finding comfort in taking in the nicotine, feeling some of the stress start to disappear. The seconds of relaxation became something that I craved and craved more and more. Slowly my quota each day increased, first five, then ten, up and up. I could not sit down without the tiny white stick in my hand – what a source of relief. Slowly I had reached a grand total of as many as fifty a day! My fingers looked stained and dirty. I was so ashamed of them that I would try to cover my hands if I was out in public.

My children and Glen found it difficult to cope. They could see changes in me that could not be avoided, but this was one thing which I could control. My clothes and hair smelled of cigarettes. My mouth tasted dirty. Even in bed I could not resist the pull of the one vice I had fought against for as long as I had lived.

One night, I went to bed early. Not feeling too good from the symptoms of MS, I lay in bed lighting one cigarette from the end of another, chain smoking. Indeed, eight cigarettes from going to bed at night and getting up in the morning had become a regular occurrence. I even set the blankets on fire. Glen walked in to see flames, sheets on fire. My chest was scarred where the ends of cigarettes had fallen on to it still lit. This was ridiculous. I was out of control.

So there came a point where I knew I wanted so much to stop. I thought of the use of visualisation. How could I use this tool to help me to reach my goal? I looked at a cigarette. "Yes that is it", I thought. It was white on the outside and looked so pure, it was offering me a form of escapism. However, the inside was black, full of nicotine, tar and many other destructive chemicals. It would attack my lungs, damage them, do my health no good. Yes, for a few seconds it was nice but long term it was doing damage and how long did the benefit of smoking that one cigarette last for anyway? Not very.

I had always told my children about the dangers of smoking and here I was being hypocritical. I was even smoking in front of my granddaughter. I knew I had the resources to cope without smoking.

Using this knowledge, I started my goal of quitting a habit I did not need in my life. It was not easy, the craving for nicotine was high, I felt agitated at times, but knew I had to go through this in order to get to the end. I slowly moved from smoking fifty down to forty, then to thirty.

The crazy thing was that I hung on to two cigarettes per day. I knew the answer was not to be angry with myself for still smoking a small number but to be pleased with myself for the victory. I then started to notice the skin on my fingers becoming stain free, my breath tasting better, my skin tone looking fresher. The benefits far surpassed those of hanging onto my little white stick. It was a year later when I was finally able to let go of the last two but they went and I can finally say I am a non–smoker.

My middle daughter asked me if I wanted to go swimming one night. I was so tempted to say no because I expected the cold of the water to produce severe spasms in my legs. Changes in temperature can affect the nerves in the limbs in many ways. But I realised I could get out of the pool if I suffered too much. What a wonderful night it was. The first time I had swum for years. How fantastic to get back into the pool where the girls and I had had so much fun when they were younger. How long had I let my fear prevent me from such a pleasurable night? I was doing something I enjoyed and at the same time I was having quality time with my daughter. Besides that I was exercising and finding a means of increasing my stamina. I yearned to be able to swim a mile again, which is something I used to find so easy to do.

19: PAYING FORWARD

It was at this time that Tony and his business partner Julie French were running an event called Ignite One. Each one attending would become a member of the Academy of High Achievers. The main focus of this was to teach people to look beyond their own limiting beliefs, to teach them massive goals are achievable. Also they wanted to show people how magnificent each individual is. I could not believe it when I was invited along to participate.

My excitement faded slowly as the conversation with Tony ended. I was going to be out of my comfort zone completely. Mixing with people who I had never met before scared me so much. I came up with every excuse in my mind. Then I thought, feel the fear and do it anyway! Was I going to let this opportunity pass me by for the sake of my insecurity? Not knowing how to mix with people – feeling inadequate? No way! I was going to go.

The first part of the venue took place on a Monday in September 2004 in Manchester. Thirty two delegates were there alongside several trainers and coaches... Wow! What an awesome day! I began to realise the limitations I had been placing on myself through fear of failure, or not feeling ready. The first step had been taken, and I met some wonderful people.

For anyone who is keen to experience an invaluable learning experience I would suggest you think about going on an Ignite program with Tony and Julie. On that day in question it was shown that massive goals can be met. Dreams can become reality. It is only we who can put restrictions on how much can be achieved.

Each of us had to set a big goal for ourselves.

I decided to combine my desire to swim a mile with raising money for charity. It was going to be a means of paying forward some of what had been done for me.

We often hear of trying to pay people back but paying forward is so important. You can never return the past but you can bring pleasure into people's lives. Tony knew of a charity called Child Advocacy International. They needed £11,000 to build and refurbish a mother and baby unit out in Bamenda, Cameroon. As I heard more about the project my passion to help grew.

This was the break through I needed to spur me on. I had made my decision, now it was time for action. I asked at the venue for sponsors and nobody refused.

Sally Gunnell, the renowned athlete was speaking on this particular day, to explain how she achieved *her* goals. I listened in awe. I am going to include an article, about Sally, which was submitted by a delegate on the course, Joe Armstrong. He has become a very dear friend of mine and within the article he illustrates the power of believing in being a winner, reaching the ultimate and surviving the impossible!

Body, Mind, Spirit

by Joe Armstrong

Did ye ever hear of Sally Gunnell? I admit I hadn't but you fine things having the finger on the pulse probably have. She was Olympic, Commonwealth, European and Something Else champion all in the one year. Some achievement, eh?

I met her recently in Manchester. She was speaking at an event organised by the Academy of High Achievers to people who embarked on a massive personal goal. Sally talked about her delight in discovering something she was good at. "One day I'm going to go to the Olympics," she told herself in her teens.

Like most winners she saw herself as lucky – but knew too that she made her own luck. She'd a whole group of friends interested in athletics and then one of the top athletics coaches spotted her. "I believed in my coach," she said.

She was only 14 and had to commit to training three nights a week.

"I'd set myself realistic, achievable goals at the beginning of each year," she said. Once she'd achieved them, her confidence and self–belief grew. She respected others. But she knew she was as good as them too.

Visualisation

"Seventy per cent of it is in the mind. You decide if you're going to win. I believe I'd mentally prepared myself better than they did." Such an extraordinary belief in the power of mental preparation I'd never come across before. There was Sally at the beginning of the Olympic race. She knew some others were faster than her. She knew other competitors were more skilled than her. But she knew she was going to win! Why? Because she knew that nobody else could have prepared themselves as well, mentally, as she had. As she put it, she was "force feeding myself with positive thoughts". It worked!

Listen to this: Thirty times a day for a year Sally visualised that race. I'm going to repeat that. Thirty times a day for a year she visualised the Olympic race! She'd see herself clipping a hurdle – and still winning. She'd 'watch' it in colour and in black and white. She'd visualise herself winning the race when she was down with 100 metres to go.

"I knew exactly in my mind what I wanted to achieve," she said. While practising visualisation, "Always see yourself coming first – not second," she counselled. "If I see myself coming second, I rewind the tape. But don't cross that line in second place even in your mind." She would replay her imaginary tape and 'see' where she lost the race then run it from there with the right thinking.

Wow! If you want to achieve highly at anything in life, you fine things, you couldn't do better than play it like Sally.

She knew she was in contest with herself. Her thinking would decide whether she'd get there or not. Seventy per cent of her winning was down to managing her thoughts! Yes, it bears repeating. Become aware of your thinking and you can stop losing thoughts and replace them with achieving more highly than you dared to imagine. And why not think a MASSIVE goal rather than just a little goal. Then break it down into stepping stones to reach each year. Oh, and banish excuses. Sally had a cold before one of her championship wins. She knew she had the perfect excuse not to win or even play. She could have withdrawn from the race. But she would never have known if she had been good enough to win with a cold. And win she did!

Final shot from Sally: "I used to train on Christmas day because I knew they wouldn't."

If she could win at the Olympic games and come away with medals what was stopping me? I knew the answer to that straight away it was a fear of failure! Here I was on a course teaching me it was possible to achieve goals, massive goals and I had the nerve to think that swimming a mile was out of my depth. So what if I failed? At least I would have tried. At least I would not be allowing myself to be a victim of fear, inadequacy and lack of self worth. I was going to be a winner because even if I did not manage to swim the full mile I would have tried. I asked Sally to sponsor me, got up on stage and had my photograph taken with her for the press. Commitment made.

20: Shivers Down My Spine

The next part of the Ignite programme was to take place in Scotland in a lovely area called Peebles. We were at a residential venue for six whole days, of which I will tell you in a short while. I noticed on the itinerary Sir Chris Bonington was to be a speaker, talking about his missions to climb Mount Everest. So an email was sent out to him, explaining I was going to see him at his talk in Peebles and to ask him if he would kindly sponsor me to do my swim.

You cannot imagine the delight I had when a wonderful email back from his secretary saying he would. Not only that but he would present the cheque in person when we met!

On Tuesday September 28th 2004, just three months after entering the pool for the first time I swam my mile. What a humbling experience it was because people donated and sponsored me. The following article went in the newspaper, I was really amazed when a couple of friends rang up to congratulate me.

MUM DIVES IN TO HELP GET CASH FOR CHILDREN ABROAD

A mother who has multiple sclerosis is doing a sponsored swim to raise cash for disadvantaged children.

Lynn Grocott, aged 44, of Denstone, was diagnosed with MS more than 10 years ago.

Because her condition has now worsened she has had to give up work and, on some days, is confined to a wheel chair.

She find swimming is the only form of exercise she can manage. After hearing about the work Child Advocacy International carries out in Cameroon she decided to use her hobby to help them raise the £13,000 they need to continue their work out there. Newcastle–based Child Advocacy International (CAI) has been working to help children in Cameroon overcome a particularly nasty form of cancer, Burkitt's Lymphoma.

It affects children, usually between the ages of 2 and 16, causing rapidly growing tumours, and if no treatment is given it is invariably fatal.

Successful treatment gives dramatic results, with tumours shrinking at a very fast rate. CAI's project is showing 75 per cent of children treated are now in remission.

A further £13,000 will enable the charity to set up a mother and baby unit to provide extra care. Charity organiser Meggio Szczesny said: "We think it is absolutely fantastic that she is going to take on this event for us. It will really help the children in Cameroon, particularly the children who have cancer, who cannot afford to pay the £200 course of treatment because they are so poor.

"It will also help to alleviate a lot of pain and suffering in the hospital, as we will be able to purchase more essential drugs and medical supplies.

"Anybody else who would be able to fund–raise, please get in touch."

Mrs Grocott is also working with Tony Burgess organising further fund–raising events and raffles and collecting old mobile phones. They would also be grateful if anyone has any old toys they can donate.

It sent shivers down my spine. I wanted more success, less failure, the pleasure it brought was amazing and it led to so many other fantastic things happening. My husband and children were so proud and even the lady who comes in to care for me on Monday mornings came and swam part of the swim with me! Tony Burgess gave up his entire evening to count the lengths. There were no spasms in my legs from the cold, just sheer pleasure, a freedom of movement. I could still shed tears of joy as I think about the moment I climbed out of the pool exhausted but exhilarated.

Even enough energy was left at the end of the swim to go for a drink to celebrate.

21: Do Me Proud

Now for the next challenge! It may seem such a small trivial thing but to think of travelling to Scotland without my family was scary. I needed Glen to take care of my medication. “What if I had a fall?”, “What if I had a flare up?”, “What if I could not keep up with the pace that was expected from me?”, “What if? What if? What if?” Then I thought, “What if I don’t go?” I knew I would be missing out on the chance of a lifetime.

I wonder if we ever realise how much energy can be wasted on “What if?”. Once again language plays a huge part in the way we talk to ourselves. If the “What if?” always ends with a negative then it prevents us from taking action. If we could try replacing the negative all the time with a positive... how much more would we try? How much more success would we taste? How much more would we experience things we have always dreamed of doing? How much easier would it be to reach our true potential?

Glen was an amazing tower of strength. He took me to buy some new clothes and saved some money for me, which was no easy task. There I was going to an amazing hotel whilst he stayed at home with the everyday tasks to fulfil and lots of decorating to do.

Inside my suitcase I found a small note that said, “Do Me Proud!” He was with me in thought and spirit all of the time and not once did he resent me doing what I was doing! I felt a little sad as I boarded the aeroplane, it was my first flight and I so wanted to share it with my husband. But I knew he was thinking of me and would not want me to be sad in any way.

What a fantastic experience! I was fascinated as I boarded the plane. I wanted to savour every moment. How was this huge lump of metal going to stay in the air? How high was it going to go? We taxied down the runway, the next thing I knew we were in the air. The take off was not like one of the fast rides at a theme park, as I thought it was going to be. I had no reason to cling to the seat in fear, which I thought I may do. Instead the plane climbed slowly and steadily. As I looked through the window at the clouds below me I marvelled at how the fluffy white grey masses just hung. If I could get on a plane and fly, what else could I experience if I stopped the "What if?" entering my mind. I was really looking forward to the days ahead of me. I long now to go up in a plane again and I am sure it will happen because I now know dreams can become reality if you will just let them.

Arriving at Peebles was wonderful, all of the people I met in Manchester were there giving each other a hug. It was like one big family. I will tell you a little more about this experience in a short while.

The first coach I saw was a fitness coach. Right, I thought, in for a penny in for a pound. I grabbed him and asked him if he would help me to swim two miles by the time we went home in six days time! Steve Halls took on the challenge with no hesitation whatsoever. He faithfully worked with me each morning from 5.40 until 8am teaching me to make the most of each stroke in the hotel pool.

He really knew how to work me too. The initial exercises began with ten squats every time I went to sit down anywhere. I felt such a fool, but found the squats getting easier and easier all the time. He really knew how to get people working without realising they were doing exercises. What's more he made it fun. We did so much laughing that week that my ribs hurt but I was not sure whether they hurt from laughing or from exercise. It was a sure thing I was not going to give up laughing.

The swimming pool was something special, at one end a window offered a magnificent view. As I swam towards it my eyes marvelled at the mountains, I could not think of a nicer place to be working my way to completing my second goal. The water was so warm, so clear. Now was the time to use visualisation. I knew I had taken on a massive challenge. This was twice the distance I had swum one week before. I knew I could do it if I focused really hard. I kept the window at the far end of the pool in mind, knowing how lovely it was to be swimming towards it, so every time I swam in the opposite direction, I had my favourite return length to do. The night before my swim, we had a party celebrating the last night in Peebles. There was no bed on that night for most of us. We sat chatting and singing well into the early hours in the morning.

Friday the 8th of October came, the day of the swim. Six days after arriving at Peebles, I could not believe it. Steve had arranged staggered swimmers to swim the two miles with me! The support from the whole of the group was unbelievable, those who did not swim, watched and encouraged me!

I entered the pool at five forty five in the morning, the water warm and inviting. Five lengths later and, as always, I felt stiff. My arms ached. Get through the first ten and it would wear off. Get my pace steady, now start letting myself drift into another world...

I was Sally Gunnell running the race, I could see the fans cheering – wanting me to win. Then I was an Olympic swimmer, distance no object. Breathe slowly. Stretch your arms and pull the water behind you as far as you could. Use the power of the stroke, which Steve had been working on. Try reducing the number of strokes per length. Watch your breathing. Go with the flow.

Then I imagined being on a podium receiving a medal. Then back to reality. Think about the mothers and babies in Cameroon, they need the unit so badly. Think how if you make this swim you are getting closer to your ultimate goal. Here comes the window again, that's it swim towards it, the sun is rising now over the mountains, the morning is turning from a dusk to light, look at the tops of the mountains as the mist hangs waiting for the sun to burn through it.

Just imagine the sun is shining on your back as you swim it will help you to keep warm. I could do it! I was going to do it! I could imagine the finishing line in front of me. Not long now – I was going to be a winner – I was going to achieve my massive goal. There was no doubt at all that I was going to cross the finishing line. Once again I was going to prove that all the "What ifs?" were not even worth thinking about. I needed my energy to swim not to worry. Go on, kick, stretch with all the might one has, go for gold.

Two miles were completed and once again I was elated. As Steve helped me out of the pool I looked behind me. It was like looking at the red arrows because a group of swimmers were all coming home in formation! What an amazing illustration of team work.

The comments at the bottom of this home made certificate humble me each day, they were written by one of the delegates on the course, Bryn Jones. He has faithfully offered support from the first Ignite day until today and demonstrates true loyalty, and friendship. Thank you Bryn.

I could not believe it at breakfast because Stew Evans one of the delegates borrowed one of the waiter's Scottish outfits, including kilt, dressed up in it and presented me with a carnation. He too remains a wonderful friend. Suddenly lots of good things were coming my way because Stew runs a company which supplies filters to fit to your water supply in order to drain off any impurity. He decided he wanted me to be drinking pure water at home. One day he appeared on the doorstep and installed the first part of a water filtration system, no more lime scale for me. Thank you Stew.

Another dream was to become reality too. I had always thought I would like to write a book – I had a story to tell. However, I was not sure I was creative enough. Lo and behold, there on the course was Dangerous Debbie Jenkins from Lean Marketing Press. Talk about being in the right place at the right time.

It kept happening. This could not be co–incidence – this was meant to be. I knew if I wrote a book the chance of finding the money to ever have it published would be non–existent. How wrong can someone be? There was Debs up on stage telling all of us we had a book in us.

What's more she was offering to take the gamble of publishing it. No charge to publish it. No charge to create a website. She would only take any money from sales of the book. And she was going to pay me 50% from every sale. So Debs as you read this through, I want to thank you for helping me to achieve my goal of seeing my name in print and for allowing me the chance to tell my story.

During the course of the week I shared one of my life long ambitions which has always been to swim the English channel. I was presented with the idea it may be possible to do the equivalent mileage in a swimming pool. What an inspirational thought! I could not stop thinking about it and so using my cheek (or charm) I approached Steve Halls again and asked him if he would take on the challenge of helping me reach my goal. No hesitation just a big resounding yes! Since that day he has committed himself to helping me build up my body strength with exercise.

22: Victim Or Winner? I Decide

When Steve first came to me I was still suffering with anorexia, weighing a mere 6 stones and 4 pounds. I was still concerned about gaining weight. The first thing he did was to tell me he would work with me but only if he kept the exercise within safe boundaries. So on that first Tuesday, he did a quick lung function and blood pressure test. I coped well with those two issues but then out came the tape measure and the scales! My heart began to beat. I could hear it pounding. I felt sick. This was the afternoon,– I was fully clothed. His scales might weigh differently to mine. What if I was right? What if someone had been messing about with my own scales? The blood seemed to be pumping around my body at a rate of knots. "Why do we need the scales Steve? Do we have to do the scales? Surely weight does not matter."

In order to do things safely he needed to know my weight so he could tailor the exercises to suit. I took off my watch and socks. I was shaking inside and the room began to swim. I could feel sweat starting to trickle down my back. Victim or winner? Victim or winner? Which was I going to be? Come on Lynn step forward, come on, come on. I felt my heart stop just for a minute as I lifted one foot onto the scales. I lifted my second foot, letting it stay in the air for just a second. Anything to postpone the inevitable from happening. Surely I had got the resources to do this. The words resounded in my ears, "Feel the Fear and Do it Anyway." Slowly my left foot came in contact with the scales, the whole process seemed to last for an eternity.

My body mass index was measured and my weight. Steve just looked and shook his head. He gave me exercises to do for the week. I was determined by the time he came each week that I would have finished the course he set for me. But I found I could not do as much as I wanted to do. I felt so weak. I knew I had to eat more but I had the recurring problem of indigestion making it difficult to eat the amount I needed to keep up my strength. My stomach had shrunk so much – so now, as well as it being an emotional challenge to eat it was also a huge physical challenge too.

The next three weeks were not spent exercising but discussing nutrition. I think he began to feel like a stuck record because he had to go over and over the same thing. He explained that I was not going to complete my goal unless I consumed food. His words were, "food is your friend." Those words are now written in magnetic letters on my fridge. "Eat a rainbow every day," is another saying Steve liked. Imagine seeing a rainbow on your plate instead of a mountain of food. A pot of gold at the end of my rainbow would be to be able to exercise more and to reach my dream goal of swimming further and further – and with ease. Steve compiled a diet sheet for me, which at the time scared me so much that I almost vomited at the sight of it.

I was having difficulty coping with small amounts let alone coping with a diet sheet. I wondered how I was ever going to beat this hurdle. Back in my mind I searched, longing to break free of another string which I had attached myself to. Notice something here, I had become attached to the string. The string didn't attach itself to me and therefore I could be free – I was in control. If this was the case then I had to decide if I wanted to be free of this problem, or if I was going to let it rule me and control me.

I thought back to Peebles and remembered... *I* decide. I can feel the fear and do it anyway.

I made a mental checklist of all of the consequences of continuing to restrict my food intake and losing even more weight. Then I made a list of the benefits of eating properly and becoming healthy.

Not eating	Eating sensibly
Feeling cold	Feeling warm
Feeling weak	Feeling strong
Aching bones	Healthy bones
No energy	Energy to swim

Language once again played a huge part in how I looked at consumption of a healthy well balanced diet. Not eating was proving to be a futile exercise –

eating properly had all the benefits I wanted.

In the initial stages of eating properly again it was horrid. The deformity of the kitchen cupboards, the way my mind lied to me. The most apt way I can describe it is like living in a hall of mirrors. I remember thinking I look fat, ugly, like a freak. I knew there was no way I could trust myself. As I walked past mirrors I avoided looking at myself so I did not allow my mind to distort the image looking back at me. When anyone gave me a hug I still felt big.

I began to realise it didn't matter how I felt. I was not the person who was giving me a hug and as long as *they* felt they wanted to hug me I must be all right. I checked my morals. Was I going to let this thing compromise me any more? I had lied too much, yes I who loved honesty had covered up my illness with lies. I had through my back teeth about the amount I had eaten – I had lied to myself and to those who cared. But this was still so hard. My appetite was reduced. I'd fought against the need for food for so long that my body had changed.

Glen's favourite saying was ringing constantly in my mind. "The body is like a battery, you cannot keep taking out unless you top it up. It will just run flat." How true his words are and how I believe them.

Steve appeared one Tuesday to go through our exercise routine. I always looked forward to his visits. I enjoyed being able to show him I had completed my homework for the week; showing him the difference in my arm muscles through working on my upper body strength. We started the warm up exercises. I knew it was going to be hard this week. I had been struggling so much to escape the hall of mirrors. I did not want to disclose how little I had eaten on that particular morning but as we started, lifting the weight in my hand, flexing the muscle, everything was aching. I felt so weak – so tired. Everything was burning inside. The room was spinning. My heart was beating as though it was going to burst out of my chest. The room went grey, I pushed and pushed myself; I could not give in. I had a small fit, and just collapsed in a heap.

All I had eaten had been about six spoonfuls of cereal during the morning. I was nothing but selfish. This fit could have quite easily been a lot more serious. The worst thing was it was self–inflicted. I was unable to move for about five minutes. I still had to conceal how ill I felt. I had really broken the rules. It was a philosophy set by Steve that one must keep exercise safe. I had willingly broken the most important rule of all.

Then one Sunday morning as I got up to face the day, I looked at the chores in front of me and even a dish in the sink looked like a mountain of washing up! How was I going to get through the day? I barely had the energy to sit upright. My life was being over ruled and worst of all *I* was allowing this to happen – making it happen. A still small voice kept creeping in when I would least expect it... "Victim or winner? Victim or winner?" The voice became louder and louder during the course of the day. It had got lots to say to me.

My five–year–old granddaughter appeared through the door. I was so tired. That little face looked up at me, "Come on Nanna, come on what shall we do? Can we paint? Listen to my song. Read me a story. Come on Nanna, come on, come on. Let's make a cake"

I looked down, my little princess stood there beaming up at me, waiting expectantly. We played and when she went home I was exhausted – drained. The voice in my head started again, "Victim or winner? Victim or winner?"

It was time to really question myself. I looked inside and for the first time I began to realise I was harming my own body! It had been a shock when the neurologist diagnosed MS. I had been devastated when he told me the news, worried about the impact it would have on my body, and yet here I was abusing the body I was so worried about. I was allowing myself to become weak. It was I who refused to take in energy. I was being so selfish and my actions were having an impact on the people I loved too.

23: GETTING STRONGER

Just think... If I had achieved the two–mile swim on such a small amount of fuel, how much more I could be doing if I allowed my body what it needed to work properly? I was depriving my family of the energetic person I knew I could be. Things had to change. It was not going to be easy but I had felt the fear before over many things and now I knew I had to feel it again. There was no escaping it. I really had to take that step to conquer it, and the step had to be taken now.

I looked at the diet sheet Steve had compiled for me. He had made his promise, "Fit people do not get fat." I thought about the comment in an email from him.

"I will not let you get fat, it would be no good for you and it would be no good for my business!" Suddenly I realised I could no longer trust my own judgement as regards to my own body size but I had to trust someone else. I needed someone, who was distant from me in terms of relationship, and also someone who would be completely honest. It would not have worked had I used Glen to be my judge, as I knew logically he would be honest, but illogic told me, "Of course he will tell you that you are not fat. He wants you to be happy." He would not have for one minute done this, because he also knows the disadvantages of being over weight, but he was too close.

Steve had a vested interest in me. His business revolved around fitness and health. If I was over weight it would not bring him good publicity. He needed me to be looking and feeling my best, so I decided to take the first step of making a concerted effort not to lose another pound. It may not seem like a massive leap forward to anyone who has not suffered with an eating disorder, but for those who have any knowledge of the illogical impact this illness can have on the mind, they'll know that the step was MASSIVE. What's more I was never hungry anymore. I was going to have to force food down. The challenge was staring me in the face. Once again I asked myself what I had to lose if I did not accept the test and compared what I had to gain if I took the bull by the horns and grasped the task with both hands. When I compared the two answers the conclusion was that eating gave so many positives...

- Energy
- Vitality
- Health
- Victory
- Helping Others
- Feeling Well

Nothing I could think of would allow me to see any reason for holding on to the anorexia. So I looked on the task as another challenge. I knew the journey could be as easy or as hard as I made it. I had to find a way of accepting myself, embracing myself and realising that all the talk in the world was not going to get me what I wanted. Only action could do that!

Yes, this was what I wanted, but how could I change the amount of fear I was feeling, the panic, the addiction? Yes, addiction! How did I know I was going to feel panic until I made the move? What would happen if I practiced with a small amount each day, I could always stop if it was too much to cope with. Then I looked at the tools I had mastered to give me coping skills. Surely there were some which could help here. I focused on the swimming I wanted to do. I knew I would not achieve any more long swims if I didn't practice and I wouldn't be strong enough to practice if I didn't eat. Food is my friend! Food is my friend! Yes, food could be my friend. It could enable me to reach my goal. I could make this as easy or as difficult as I chose to make it.

I developed an image in my mind of an old–fashioned kitchen scale. To be the right weight to do my swimming I needed to be seven stones and seven pounds. Anything below was unbalanced and anything too much above that weight was also unbalanced. In my mind I visualised my scales and the balance was not there. I was well below the target of seven stones and seven pounds. I was six stones and four pounds. I had to make a start.

Tuesday the 30th November saw the end of a three mile swim. This again was an amazing, magical experience, once again the word was out, people came from the Academy of High Achievers to swim with me or to watch. I used visualisation so much on this particular night. My dear friend Joe Armstrong had told me he had lit a candle of hope in Ireland for me and was leaving it burning for the length of time I was in the pool. The deep end of the pool was so much colder than the shallow end, so as I swam toward the colder water I started to visualise the candle burning from Ireland. A lovely warm flame glowed. Just look at the way friends were pulling together so selflessly to help me reach my goal. I could not have done it without them! Thank you to all of you from Ignite. You are all amazing people!

I was starting to see how much happier I was by achieving goals. So I started to email people. With the goal of a channel swim in front of me I wanted to find some one to help with swimming techniques.

> I am a forty four year old lady who suffers with a severe form of multiple sclerosis. Three months ago I managed to start swimming again after having spent many months in a wheel chair.
>
> Swimming is the easiest form of exercise for me and as such I decided to swim for a charity known as Child Advocacy International. Our aim is to raise over eleven thousand pounds in order to build and refurbish a mother and baby unit in Cameroon.
>
> A month ago I managed to swim a mile, which raised over four hundred pounds for the charity and then within a week I managed to increase my swimming to two miles. I am now planning a five mile swim in February 2005 and to swim the equivalent of the channel in Oct 2005. I am looking for anyone who would be willing to make a pledge to this charity or to sponsor me or make a donation when I undertake the very big swim.
>
> I am going to do this in the safety of a swimming pool because of the limitations of the multiple sclerosis.
>
> I have had some fantastic encouragement from a coach called Steve Halls. Further information can be gained about the charity by contacting my very dear friend Mr Tony Burgess.
>
> Thank you so much for reading this.

Yours truly,
Lynn Grocott

This was sent to Total Immersion Swimming. They are well known for coaching, especially in terms of swimming the length of the channel.

When the reply came back that they would offer professional swimming coaching I could hardly believe what was happening.

My name is Nicki and I am one of the TI coaches. Your details were passed onto me by Kevin Millerik and as I understand it you need training for a pool based channel swim?

I am based in Leicestershire, but travel extensively with my job and would be happy to discuss your requirements and how I can help. It sounds like you have the same independent drive as my Mum (she has had rheumatoid for nearly 40 years and more operations than I can remember). She doesn't let anything stop her and has recently learnt to swim battling against physical restrictions and a strong fear of water!

It amazes me how strong people like you and her are and what you selflessly achieve.

Best wishes

Nicola

Can you see? The result of taking on challenges head to head was reaping rewards in such a positive way! No longer are people saying to me, "Oh, I do feel sorry for you, it must be awful!" But I am now finding people are coming from all walks of life to help me reach my goals.

They are starting to see determination in me and a source of hidden strength. They are starting to see someone who is prepared to fight for what she wants. This feeling far surpasses the feeling of being a good cause or a victim.

I still found myself struggling with the food though. Some days were easier than others. I knew logically I could not maintain the exercises without the intake of food. My taste buds had changed so much – nothing tasted nice. I suffered with chronic stomach pains when I ate. I was managing cereal, but this was about my limit. I felt uncomfortably full and bloated, even after a few mouthfuls. I was still afraid of the scales, however, I had noticed one positive move. I was eating my breakfast every day. I was only weighing myself once each day. I was having the odd day where weight was not the first and last thing on my mind.

More important and exciting things were happening! I wanted a part of all these things. I needed energy to survive, but I did not want to *just* survive – no – I wanted to LIVE!

You have seen the photograph of me when I completed my two mile swim at Peebles. Now as I look at it some of the memory of success is removed by the sight of my figure or lack of it! I looked so gaunt, so thin – like a skeleton. Up until now I did not accept in my mind this was a photograph of me. I did not think I was so thin, more importantly I did not feel thin. In fact far from it, I still felt fat. I had completely exhausted Glen by now. Can you imagine what it is like for a loved one to see their partner on the road to self–destruction? He once asked me how I could equate love with slowly killing myself.

Self destruction may seem an emotive term to use, however, it is the truth. Anorexia can lead to heart, kidney and other types of organ failure. Anaemia, low potassium – even death. Karen Carpenter a famous singer and such a beautiful looking young lady is an example of such a tragedy. I already knew what it was like to experience losing both parents through suicide. I knew there was no way on this earth I was going to allow *my* children to have to cope with the trauma that comes from the consequences of such an act.

I was starting to overcome it in a small way. And what's more I had also started to use exercise in a new way too. Yes, I was not only reaching a point of being able to sever another string but I was finding a way of turning something destructive for the person with an eating disorder, into something positive. Anorexics are known to use exercise as a means of controlling their weight. In rehabilitation clinics exercise is not allowed until you eat a certain amount of calories each day. In my case it was the realisation of how physically weak I felt that started to hit me really hard. I had made my commitments; I wanted to carry them through so much.

Each day was still difficult in terms of eating. I had started as I meant to go on but I knew it was not going to be easy. It was going to take perseverance, determination and help from others. I knew it was possible to get well. With any addiction there are many factors involved. I had overcome other things – so this was not going to defeat me. I needed to find other ways of dealing with it. I had my weekly challenge of improving my stamina and exercise routine with Steve. I was feeling quite pleased when I looked back at how much more I was able to do in one go compared to when we first started to train together. I could not do one sit up and yet I was improving day by day. I was feeling so much healthier.

Then the answer struck me. I was still insecure – I still felt as though I had to prove myself to others. I felt the need to change for *other* people – I was still acting like a puppet in many ways. In order to free myself from anorexia and from future problems similar to it there was no other answer other than finding a way to accept myself – a way to embrace myself. I started to realise all the talk in the world was not going to get me where I needed to go, Only action could!

Once again I could see another frog croaking in front of me then I thought of the words a friend had once said: "It's important to keep the positives in mind at difficult points in life. They are a bit like a suit of armour: it can only protect you if it is well maintained and if you wear it to fend off challenges. Don't leave it rusting in the corner."

24: STANDING OVATION

I said earlier I would return to the story of the Ignite event at Peebles. I was so privileged to meet so many fantastic delegates and coaches. Amongst the coaches was a professional speaker called David Hyner. This man had, and still has, an awesome reputation, presenting talks on the Massive Goal Principle. I saw him in action and decided *I* wanted to speak in public. I wanted to tell my story to people in order to help them to realise they could overcome challenges in *their* lives.

My initial thoughts were I was doing Okay. I had started to achieve things. But it came as such a shock when David and I talked one night. He asked me when I was going to start talking like a victor rather than a victim. Shell–shocked I looked at him with my bottom lip quivering. He explained that I told my story as though I were trying to gain a sympathy vote instead of telling people how to do things through determination. I frequently mumbled about my lack of self worth, always looking for acceptance. "No good talking about lack of self worth," he said "Start believing in yourself. People want to see someone who has faith in themselves. They want to see someone who is so sure of their own self worth they are not worried about other people's opinions."

He said the most important step was to like yourself and then you could like others. I had heard this statement so many times before. Glen had told me on so many occasions I had to start to love myself. He used the words of a song to illustrate this point "Life is not worth a damn until I can say I am what I am!" In other words I had to learn to accept myself – warts and all. I began to realise I had still not conquered the biggest challenge I had ever faced. Self condemnation came too easily. I looked at myself and I could not say I liked myself. Yes *liked* myself. It might sound conceited to like yourself but it isn't. You don't have to become the sort of person who loves to be heard over everyone else or loves all the attention but you do have to accept and like yourself.

I looked again, I wanted so much to show others it was possible but had I achieved anything significant enough?

I had not been up Mount Everest like Sir Chris Bonington had. I had not sailed around the world. I hadn't beaten my competitors to claim Olympic gold. Then an email came from Sir Chris. His words were, "You have climbed Many Everests." He was right. I could give people an insight into the challenges faced in life. Maybe I could help people see a way out of their darkness. Show them that they have the resources to deal with whatever challenge they are facing too.

And what a challenge this was to become. Dave had said his piece and I thought of all the times Glen had said the same words, suddenly I knew I had to start believing I was worthy of living; worthy of love. I thought about snowflakes and how we marvel that no one snowflake is like any other. But how many of us acknowledge, really acknowledge, how unique we are as individuals, look at the human fingerprint, each one of us has a fingerprint unique to us. If each of us is unique, then each one of us is special. Each of us has something of value to share. I had got to give myself a quick hefty kick into gear.

I began to develop a genuine sense of worth. I started to realise I had achieved so much in my life. It was not an easy lesson to learn. During the course of the next two days my mind worked overtime. I had to get my story out because I wanted to show other people that it was possible to overcome challenge and adversity in their lives. I did not want people to feel sorry for me – I wanted them to see a person who they could admire; someone who they could look at and think, "if she can do it, so can I!"

I had to learn a new approach, I had to find a way of standing tall and talking with conviction. I did not want people to feel desperate during challenging times but I wanted them to see hope.

Dave must have seen a change because he went on to ask me to do my first ever public speech at an event with him on December 10th 2004 in Birmingham at Aston Villa football club. Yes, I was given my chance to talk about overcoming challenge and adversity. I knew how important this chance was. Once I had delivered my speech there was no going back – it had to show conviction – it had to show strength. I was being offered a chance to touch people's lives and I wanted to make sure I didn't blow it!

I stayed at his house the night before and I was so lucky to share the evening not only with Dave but also his wife. I don't for one minute think things happen by chance in this world. I did not realise how important a role Dave's wife was going to play in my life, but lo and behold we bonded so well. Little did I know I was in the right place at the right time again because I was to start another part of my journey.

I was so amazed when on the day of the speech I received a standing ovation from twenty people.

However, there was to be one problem which took the joy out of that particular day. I felt so physically ill. I wanted so badly to come home during the day, feeling sick and weak I wore a mask to stop the world from seeing the enormous battle I still had to face. It was a big thing I could not address in this talk. I could not say with conviction I had completely overcome anorexia because I had not, I wanted to but wanting to, starting to (which I had), and actually being able to say I *have* beaten anorexia are miles apart.

What did it mean to enjoy food? I could not understand why the indigestion when I ate was still so painful nor why my stomach felt bloated. Surely, it should not be so physically painful to eat?

I had to do something and do something quick. I spent a long time talking to Dave and Liz that night. Dave told me that my first step had got to be honesty. He said no one would judge me for being honest but lies were just not on.

"Lies" the word just resounded in my mind. Was I still lying? Were there still things I was not admitting? Yes, there were still times when I was not being one hundred percent honest with myself and in not being honest with myself I was certainly not being honest with others. If I was not careful I was still in danger of allowing my love of honesty to be taken away from me? Was I going to be stripped of a vital moral? How could I tell my story of victory without tackling this final issue?

Right! It was time once again. I addressed the issue, looked at everything and when I had. I got to feel the fear and do something about the gremlins which were left behind. It was time to conquer another puppet master!

I had to start recognising my own worth in such a way I would not have to look for reassurance all the time. I was not sure how I could reach a point where I liked myself. That night Dave gave me an exercise to do. To fill an A4 piece of paper with all the massive achievements I had made in my life. Not only to fill one side but both sides of the paper. After talking to him on the phone, I looked at the paper – it frightened me. I could not see anything at that moment in time because I was so swamped with having another challenge to sort out.

However – I took the victim cap off and the winner took over. Soon I had compiled a few things in a list. Emailing them I felt quite proud, until the reply came back. Dave had seen straight through me. He saw I had written my achievements but in such a way that I was not convinced within myself that they were worthy of recognition. Back to the drawing board. As I wrote now, I digested the words, looked at them as if I were reading about someone else and suddenly realised I had achieved massive things.

Overcoming physical and sexual abuse, turning it on its head, bringing up three children to know the true value of love... Wow! No mean task. The list grew, and as I wrote I started to feel the sense of self worth rising within me.

I noticed with the growth of self worth came a different attitude to everything. I would say it is something I am still learning and as I learn each day, I become more and more confident, more at ease. As my self worth grew I could see more and more positives each day. I noticed how I had started to really feel much safer eating now –

instead of having to eat under duress. I started to find I looked forward to small amounts of food for breakfast.

25: Fighting Anorexia

Initially the physical pain of digesting food was not pleasant. I felt so full even after six small spoonfuls. I had professional insight through Liz. She knew how many calories I needed just to lie in bed each day. I was still consuming nowhere near that amount. I accepted it was going to be a slow thing because I could not stand being bloated and I realised I had to allow my digestive system to start working again. Everything had slowed down – even my stomach had stopped properly breaking down the food it was consuming.

Liz explained that my stomach was like a paper bag, when I ate it swelled but would go down again. It had shrunk so much over time, it needed to be treated with love and care.

Liz was amazing. She emailed me most days to see how I was. In her role as a friend she knew she had taken on a massive commitment. Directing me to the EDA website (www.edauk.com) was an inspiration. I would recommend this website to carers, suffers, professionals and anyone with an interest in learning more about preventing this illness.

The main thing was to have a tempting choice in the house and I was so lucky Glen was prepared to go to any length to ensure choice was there. Plain biscuits became easy to digest and I was soon managing a small amount of cooked vegetables.

Granted in the very beginning some days were easier than others, but Glen was wonderful. He never pressurised me now, he left me to decide when to eat and how much. I know these were difficult days for him and I know he suffered greatly with worry. He stood by me – always ready to pick up the pieces if things went wrong. What an amazing tower of strength. What a partner! How blessed I was and still am to have him.

Glen bought vitamin tablets, making sure I got one each morning. He was trying to do all he could. I began to notice I was slowly gaining strength and energy. I was going to have the energy to complete this book! It was amazing because at one point I thought I had bitten off more than I could chew. I could not concentrate or remember things because of lack of food, but now I was writing more and more.

Ideas were coming thick and fast. I was seeing the beauty of nutrition. I had literally starved not only my body but my brain too. I had been wasting time because all I wanted to do before I started to eat again was to sleep. How many wasted hours? I could never regain the time, but I could make sure I did not go down the same path again.

However, I had one problem, I could not get rid of indigestion. I knew I was not being difficult. This was not an excuse to hang on to anorexia. I had made my decision and I was going to stick to it. But my weight was not increasing – it was staying the same or falling. Everyone looked at me with questioning eyes. Surely this was not the sign of someone who was trying to get over anorexia. I could see their worry.

My own actions in the past had caused the doubt in other people. I could not blame them for doubting.

At times I could not get comfortable. I was using a hot water bottle on my stomach because my ribs were so painful. Spasms made me feel as though my chest was crushing me; it was difficult to breathe. I had pain in my back. Then I started to question *myself.* I asked myself if my subconscious had taken over. I now know the impact that it can have over the way we act, think and believe so I was forced to tap into it. I had to ask myself if this was just me – developing a means of remaining an anorexic? I knew the truth. I wanted to be free from anorexia – I wasn't playing tricks on myself.

There were no issues that had been left to crop up unawares. The truth of the matter was I really wasn't hungry. Drinking a full cup of fluid was difficult – feelings of nausea flooded my body. Burning pains in my stomach. However, people around me, understandably, thought I was just being awkward – wanting to hang on to anorexia. This was not true – I was really suffering physically. It was terrible to see the faces of disbelief as I told them how I felt.

I went to my GP –even he looked doubtful but then he thought the problem was due to acid forming in the stomach and as such prescribed tablets to settle it.

Eventually I was admitted into hospital – my blood count showed how low my haemoglobin level was and I received three pints of blood. Several scans were done and the CT scan revealed a dilated bile duct which is indicative of many physical illnesses. The initial thought was there was a blockage or even a tumour near to the pancreas. Yes –a cancer scare.

26: It's Okay To Fail

As the consultant left my bedside having talked about the thoughts he had. I was afraid and I was faced with looking at my own mortality. I knew cancer in the pancreas was not something to be taken lightly.

I spoke to Dave that night. He asked me why I was afraid. It was obvious surely! As we spoke I realised I was afraid of something which had not even been confirmed. I was expecting the worst. I was doing it again I was thinking, "what if?" Turn it around I thought, "What if it isn't cancer?" Or at times I would think, "What if it is cancer, how can I fight it, because other people do? Other people beat cancer... if they can then I can."

It was not easy to do. I would sometimes catch myself having a moment where the positive thoughts went away to be drowned by the fear. But at least I knew the fear was not going to overwhelm me. It was not going to take the fight away from me. I was going to use the strength of the fear emotion to help me.

Yes, fear is a strong all encompassing emotion, it uses up so much energy but I was going to have fear working for me. I was going to employ fear and I was going to make it become inspiration to fight. No matter what – I was going to fight and fight with all my strength.

I went through several days of being afraid, then I addressed my fear, knowing that no matter what, I could cope as long as the pain was under control. Thankfully another test revealed there was no tumour and so on to other investigations.

Apparently one of the most common causes of a dilated bile duct is chronic pancreatitis, or inflammation of the pancreas. I am still undergoing tests and am still fighting this one battle today. I know once they have got the pain control sorted I will cope and continue to live life in the way I want to.

I have had to really digest the words of Chris Bonington, "It is alright to fail." because I did not complete my five mile swim in February.

But it doesn't matter. I know the swim will be done when it is right to do it. In the meantime I had to put the final touches to this book.

Prior to going into hospital Glen and I looked at the medication I was taking for MS. The list was long. I had been on some of these drugs for years. He explained to me some of the drugs were so sedative in nature. He wondered if I could manage to reduce any of them, and in doing so become less tired. Was there a chance I could drive again? Anything was possible. Even if it did not result in me being able to return to driving, surely I would feel better without them inside me. So Glen encouraged me to think about reduction.

Clonazepam is a very powerful drug, it is in the same family as diazepam but much stronger. Besides helping keep the spasms and the spasticity of the muscles under control, it is highly addictive. I knew I was dependent on this drug. The psychological dependence could be as strong as the physiological. I asked Glen to take control of the reduction. I was taking eight tablets each day. How nice it would be to be free of this one drug – to only use it when things were at their worst. At the moment, if things became worse I could not take any extra medication and severe pain was so difficult to treat with pain killers because my body was so used to large heavy amounts of medication. Let's face it – nothing could be as bad as what I had experienced when withdrawing from harsh drugs in years gone by. I suppose I was worried in case the pain came back from the MS. Silly irrational fear creeping in again; assumptions being made without evidence.

Glen agreed he was prepared to monitor the drops, he did not tell me when he had cut one of the tablets out.

Dropping the Clonazepam by a quarter of a tablet at a time. In a couple of weeks of writing this book it is one drug which I shall no longer be taking. I admit there are times when the spasms are there – but pain is something which we adjust to. I still suffer fatigue – I still have bad days – but I now know I can help myself to deal with pain in a better way. It is wonderful to now I am in control of what drugs I take. They do not control me, they have no hold on me.

I am not saying drugs do not have their part to play. They do. But what had happened in my case was I had just not considered reducing my drugs in accordance with how the MS was affecting me.

Even before going to Ignite, before experiencing the hurdles in life which had to be cleared, I knew humans were incredible beings. Both gifted and talented. I have thought on many occasions how capable we all are.

If we push ourselves it is surprising – the results we find. Go back to the patient in the hospital where I worked who could clear himself and the chair off the ground – think of his physical strength. He used it because he did not think about limits. In the same way as a child is not limited in learning to walk. It is we who impose our limited view of life's boundaries. On our children.

How much more could we achieve if we could become more like children in our thinking and imagining? Think of the places my imagination was capable of taking me when I was dressed in my football strip – there were no limits. I could be whoever I wanted to be – do whatever I put my mind to do. I could be famous – I could climb mountains.

Put imagination and determination together, you can have an incredible combination. Then harness the power of fear, and put it to work for you. Then you have in front of you three powerful tools which can be turned into real energy – an energy that enables you to cope with and overcome anything life has to offer.

So what now? I think the main thing is I can now see challenge in a totally different light. I am not for one minute trying to say I don't get upset, or have an odd bad day. This book is not about that. The message is to say to you that anything is possible. You have to believe it. You have to make your subconscious believe it. I am now living for today. Happiness comes from within.

I am happy with who I am. No one can take that away from me. Whatever you are going through – there is always light at the end. If you have a dream, an ambition or a goal then go for it. Action can turn thoughts into reality. You may decide in a change of direction as you start to build on your goals, it does not matter. Go in the direction that feels right for you and you simply cannot fail.

After all – you decide. Don't be controlled – don't be a puppet to other people or circumstance. Be master of your own destiny. Bad situations can be changed to good. You are stronger than you could ever imagine. You are resourceful. You are a unique individual. I hope today may be the start of you're an even better life. I hope your dreams will take you into the world of achieving massive goals. If they do then this book will have served its purpose.

27: THE ARROW BREAK

Expecting a normal morning of lectures, I was shocked.

In front of me were three maniacs. They were telling me it was possible to break a metal tipped arrow by putting it on my epiglottis. They were allowing someone to hold the arrow firmly to my neck with a thick board, and then telling me if I walked closer and closer to the arrow pressing more and more so that the arrow pushed harder and harder into my throat, I could break it without it doing me any damage at all.

The trick was performed in front of me. We were asked if we felt comfortable trying it. No pressure they said. No pressure? And the people around me – people I thought were pretty much sane – were agreeing to do it too.

Fools I thought, this is no joke, they mean it! These people around me really mean it. They're about to kill off thirty–odd delegates! This is time to run!

Then I looked at Tony Burgess, yes I knew him, he wanted to live, yet he had got an arrow in his hand. I looked at his business associate Julie, yep she is lovely I thought, but then she was wild, anything for a challenge, maybe she was going too far in the course of duty today.

Then I thought about it. I thought about all the times when fear had worked against me not so long ago. The fear which had stopped me from swimming until I got back into the pool.

In for a penny in for a pound. I placed the arrow to my throat, not too bad at the moment and then the pressure as the arrow and the board became closer. I looked at this logically for a fleeting second. I could always move back if I wanted to. No chance! I allowed the panic to well up inside me and the uncomfortable feeling was somehow fading. I felt determination – I could feel my teeth clenching. I knew I could do it. Yes I knew fear was so strong but I was once again utilising its power to work for me. Snap! The arrow broke before I had even the slightest chance of pulling back. Yes I had broken the arrow.

When looking back I have been in so many dark places, but each time something new has been learned. I was inspired when a friend of mine sent me a quote from a Stephen King novel. For me it sums up perfectly how the past can sometimes catch up with us...

So do we pass the ghosts that haunt us later in our lives; they sit undramatically by the roadside like poor beggars, and we see them only from the corners of our eyes, if we see them at all. The idea that they have been waiting there for us rarely if ever crosses our minds. Yet they do wait, and when we have passed, they gather up their bundles of memory and fall in behind, treading in our footsteps and catching up, little by little.

Stephen King
Wizard and Glass

The demons and the ghosts may wait, they may catch us up but what do we do? Do we allow them to haunt us or do we sever their strings? Take the points below to help you decide.

Ten Tips For Cutting The Strings of Your Puppet Master

1) Never try to deal with WHAT IF? Always deal with FACT
2) Overcoming is much healthier for you than overwhelming. The next challenge won't seem as bad. You will know you are much stronger and resourceful every time you overcome something.
3) Wishing things were different doesn't work. Action does.
4) Inspirational action becomes a magnet for drawing inspirational people into your life. The more you help yourself – the more help you'll receive
5) Determination is a key factor in any challenging situation.
6) Explore every positive opportunity. Even the most challenging circumstances contain a gift for you.
7) Control all that can be controlled. Influence all that can be influenced and stop worrying about that which is beyond your control. You'll deal with it if it happens.
8) Independence does not mean you have to be alone.
9) Don't be afraid to fail but make sure you hop right back into action. It's not over until it's over.
10) Embrace challenge. You are going to become stronger and even more resourceful as a result.

NEVER FORGET THE CHALLENGE. LEARN FROM IT AND REMEMBER YOU CAN SAY “NOW I DECIDE” WHETHER TO SURVIVE AS A VICTIM OR LIVE AS A WINNER.

And so today as I submit this book to my publisher I can now rightfully claim my place as a member of the Academy of High Achievers. I have applied the principles we learned and literally achieved my massive goals.

I hope to have demonstrated to you that it *is* possible to achieve things that I once thought were dreams. You can move from victim to victor. It shows the Lynn Grocott as she is today as opposed to the Lynn Grocott from months ago.

What is most amazing is that once the shift in outlook started the changes in my life became immense. And alongside the vast changes, came speed. When I look at the time scale even I sit and look with awe.

EPILOGUE

To sum it up...

I am out of a wheelchair and have a totally different way of looking at the everyday challenges of MS. I never worry about what the illness may bring. I cope with the facts of the illness not the "What if?" I know all of the challenges MS can bring however, I know I have the resources within me to cope with whatever it may bring.

I am now an author.

I can swim three miles.

I feel self worth and know I deserve to feel worthy.

I accept that I was abused but I am not going to let it affect the rest of my life. It happened, it was something which as a child I had no control over it, but I am in control over the impact it has on my life now.

I am not to blame. I learned to ensure I turned it round for my own children and I have ensured their lives have been happy and full of love.

The suicide of my parents happened, they have gone. I can remember my parents and they chose to leave this world. I had no control over their choice but I do have a choice over the way their death affects my *life*.

I can choose to do anything I set my heart on doing.

I am not afraid to change direction in life. sometimes, as I work through the process of achieving a goal, something may lead in another direction and take on some importance in my life. As long as it brings happiness I will pursue it.

One other thing which is not to be ignored in my story is my faith. Without that my journey would have been even harder. I was touched with the comments a friend emailed to me which said...

Your comments remind me of the words of St. Paul "I can do all things through Christ who is my strength."

Every Blessing in Christ,

Graham

Dr Shevlin made me smile too when I received this email just as I was finishing this book...

Lynn! Well done! Amazing! You always had it in you to do these things...forgive me that I didn't always help in the best way. I've loads of Public Speaking stuff – in fact I've got to decide whether to renew my membership soon. I'll send on some material and just let me know if it's any use.

Congratulations and best wishes

Bernard

Dr Bernard Shevlin

This book would not have been written if my family had not encouraged me to do so. In closing I would say to them I love you dearly. The love, support and care you have given to me at all times has never been taken for granted and there is not a day goes by when I do not thank the Lord I have you in my life.